VOLUME 2

JOANNA COLE TO JACK GANTOS

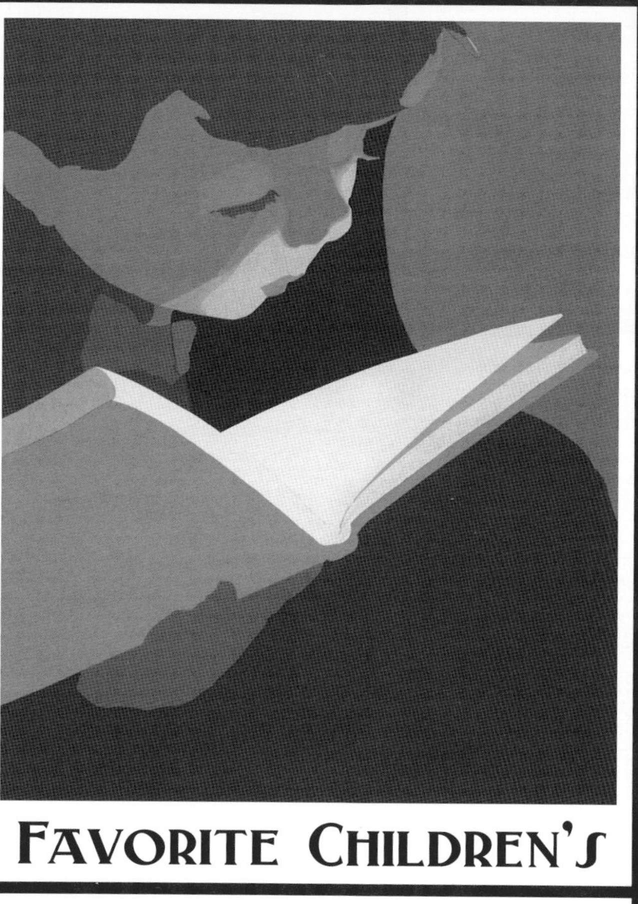

FAVORITE CHILDREN'S AUTHORS AND ILLUSTRATORS

E. RUSSELL PRIMM III, EDITOR IN CHIEF

TRADITION BOOKS™
EXCELSIOR, MINNESOTA

For Irene Barron Keller, whose love of the English language touched the lives of millions of young readers through her writing and editing

Published by **TRADITION BOOKS**™ and distributed to
the school and library market by **THE CHILD'S WORLD**®
P.O. Box 326, Chanhassen, MN 55317-0326
800/599-READ
http://www.childsworld.com

A NOTE TO OUR READERS:

The publication dates listed in each author or illustrator's selected bibliography represent the date of first publication in the United States.

The editors have listed literary awards that were announced prior to August 2002.

Every effort has been made to contact copyright holders of material included in this reference work. If any errors or omissions have occurred, corrections will be made in future editions.

Photographs ©: Candlewick Press: 28, 72; de Grummond Children's Literature Collection, University of Southern Mississippi: 16 (Weston Woods); Harcourt: 68, 96, 128; HarperCollins Publishers: 20, 36, 40 (Nina Crews), 92 (Lauren Wojtyla), 100, 112 (Becky Mojica), 116, 152 (Merry Scully); Henry Holt and Company: 120; Houghton Mifflin Company: 48, 136 (Carlo Ontal); Hyperion Books: 80 (Louise Erdrich); Kerlan Collection, University of Minnesota: 124 (Houghton Mifflin Company), 140, 148 (Whittlesey House); Library of Congress: 52; Lois Duncan: 88; Penguin Putnam: 64, 144; Pleasant Company: 32; Roddy McDowell: 104; Scholastic: 8 (Jungsoo Kim), 12, 56 (Gill Evans), 60 (Jungsoo Kim), 84, 132.

An Editorial Directions book

LIBRARY OF CONGRESS CATALOGING-IN-PUBLICATION DATA
Favorite children's authors and illustrators / E. Russell Primm, III, editor-in-chief.
p. cm.
Summary: Provides biographical information about authors and illustrators of books for children and young adults, arranged in dictionary form. Includes bibliographical references and index.
ISBN 1-59187-018-6 (v. 1 : lib. bdg. : alk. paper)—ISBN 1-59187-019-4 (v. 2 : lib. bdg. : alk. paper)—ISBN 1-59187-020-8 (v. 3 : lib. bdg. : alk. paper)—ISBN 1-59187-021-6 (v. 4 : lib. bdg. : alk. paper)—ISBN 1-59187-022-4 (v. 5 : lib. bdg. : alk. paper)—ISBN 1-59187-023-2 (v. 6 : lib. bdg. : alk. paper) 1. Children's literature—Bio-bibliography—Dictionaries—Juvenile literature. 2. Illustrators—Biography—Dictionaries—Juvenile literature. [1. Authors. 2. Illustrators.]
I. Primm, E. Russell, 1958–
PN1009.A1 F38 2002
809'.89282'03—dc21   2002007129

Printed in the United States of America.

FAVORITE CHILDREN'S AUTHORS AND ILLUSTRATORS LIBRARY ADVISORY BOARD

EDITORIAL STAFF

Table of Contents

Major Children's Author and Illustrator Literary Awards

The American Book Award

Awarded from 1980 to 1983 in place of the National Book Award to give national recognition to achievement in several categories of children's literature

The Boston Globe–Horn Book Awards

Established in 1967 by Horn Book *magazine and the* Boston Globe *newspaper to honor the year's best fiction, poetry, nonfiction, and picture books for children*

The Caldecott Medal

Established in 1938 and presented by the Association for Library Service to Children division of the American Library Association to illustrators for the most distinguished picture book for children from the preceding year

The Carnegie Medal

Established in 1936 and presented by the British Library Association for an outstanding book for children written in English

The Carter G. Woodson Book Award

Established in 1974 and presented by the National Council for the Social Studies for the most distinguished social science books appropriate for young readers that depict ethnicity in the United States

The Coretta Scott King Awards

Established in 1970 in connection with the American Library Association to honor African-American authors and illustrators whose books are deemed outstanding, educational, and inspirational

The Hans Christian Andersen Medal

Established in 1956 by the International Board on Books for Young People to honor an author or illustrator, living at the time of nomination, whose complete works have made a lasting contribution to children's literature

The Kate Greenaway Medal

Established by the Youth Libraries Group of the British Library Association in 1956 to honor illustrators of children's books published in the United Kingdom

The Laura Ingalls Wilder Award

Established by the Association for Library Service to Children division of the American Library Association in 1954 to honor an author or illustrator whose books, published in the United States, have made a substantial and lasting contribution to children's literature

The Michael L. Printz Award

Established by the Young Adult Library Services division of the American Library Association in 2000 to honor literary excellence in young adult literature (fiction, nonfiction, poetry, or anthology)

The National Book Award

Established in 1950 to give national recognition to achievement in fiction, nonfiction, poetry, and young people's literature

The Newbery Medal

Established in 1922 and presented by the Association for Library Service to Children division of the American Library Association for the most distinguished contribution to children's literature in the preceding year

The Orbis Pictus Award for Outstanding Nonfiction

Established in 1990 by the National Council of Teachers of English to honor an outstanding informational book published in the preceding year

The Pura Belpré Awards

Established in 1996 and cosponsored by the Association for Library Service to Children division of the American Library Association and the National Association to Promote Library Services to the Spanish Speaking to recognize a writer and illustrator of Latino or Latina background whose works affirm and celebrate the Latino experience

The Scott O'Dell Award

Established in 1982 and presented by the O'Dell Award Committee to an American author who writes an outstanding tale of historical fiction for children or young adults that takes place in the New World

Joanna Cole

Born: August 11, 1944

There's a little bit of Ms. Frizzle, the wildly dressed teacher and star of the Magic School Bus series, in author Joanna Cole herself. The character, based on Joanna's favorite elementary-school science teacher, has the same love of science and children that motivated Cole to write for young readers.

Joanna Cole was born on August 11, 1944, in Newark, New Jersey. As a child, she was fascinated by gardening, insects, and animals. She was always curious about how and why things are the way they are. She also loved reading children's books, an interest that carried over into her adult life.

In school, English and science were Joanna's best subjects. Writing about science turned out to be a perfect way to combine these interests. "As a child, I enjoyed writing and I

Joanna Cole did some of the research for her first book, *Cockroaches,* in her New York City apartment, where many of the creatures scampered around right before her eyes!

wrote for the sheer fun of it. I think that's very important—not to be always looking at what the outside world will say about you," says Cole.

After finishing high school in East Orange, New Jersey, Joanna Cole attended the University of Massachusetts and Indiana University. She finally graduated from the City College of New York with a bachelor's degree in psychology.

"I had a teacher who was a little like Ms. Frizzle. She loved her subject. Every week she had a child do an experiment in front of the room, and I wanted to be that child every week!"

After college, Joanna Cole worked as a librarian in a Brooklyn elementary school, followed by a period as an elementary schoolteacher. Her first writing job was at *Newsweek* magazine. There, she answered letters to the editor.

During her years as an elementary-school librarian, Joanna Cole rediscovered her love of children's books. She left the academic world and took a job at Doubleday Books for Young Readers. After eventually working her way up to the position of senior editor, she decided to try her own hand at writing children's books. Realizing that very few books for kids are about insects—and none at all are about the dreaded cockroach—Cole began research for her first published book, *Cockroaches.*

From there, she tackled such subjects as plants, dinosaurs, frogs, horses, and cats. When an editor at Scholastic suggested that Cole

---

COLE ALWAYS CREATES A "DUMMY" MAGIC SCHOOL BUS BOOK WITH TEXT, WORD BALLOONS, ROUGH SKETCHES, AND JOKES ON SMALL STICK-ON NOTES. WHEN SHE MEETS WITH HER EDITOR, COLE PEELS OFF THE NOTES TO FIND THE JOKES THAT MAKE HER EDITOR LAUGH.

A Selected Bibliography of Cole's Work

Ms. Frizzle's Adventures: Ancient Egypt (2001)
Gator Halloween (1999)
Get Well, Gators! (1998)
The Magic School Bus in the Rain Forest (1998)
I'm a Big Brother (1997)
Rockin' Reptiles (1997)
The Magic School Bus: Inside a Beehive (1996)
How I Was Adopted: Samantha's Story (1995)
The Magic School Bus Gets Baked in a Cake: A Book about Kitchen Chemistry (1995)
The Magic School Bus on the Ocean Floor (1992)
The Magic School Bus, Lost in the Solar System (1990)
Evolution (1987)
The Magic School Bus: Inside the Earth (1987)
The Magic School Bus at the Waterworks (1986)
How You Were Born (1984)
Bony-Legs (1983)
Cars and How They Go (1983)
A Frog's Body (1980)
My Puppy Is Born (1973)
Cockroaches (1971)

Cole's Major Literary Awards

1987 *Boston Globe–Horn Book* Nonfiction Honor Book
The Magic School Bus at the Waterworks

combine science with fictional characters, the award-winning Magic School Bus series was born. Covering subjects such as the solar system, the weather, the ocean floor, and bees, the hugely popular series is well respected by educators and experts alike.

The books led to an animated series on PBS television. Students can also visit a Magic School Bus Web site to

> *"We all learn to be writers from the books we read as kids. Reading gives you a very solid feel for the language, and an understanding of how to write. When you start to write, you can use that understanding."*

explore many topics in a fun-filled way with the Magic School Bus gang.

Readers of the Magic School Bus series, with colorful illustrations by Bruce Degen, know that Joanna Cole has a great sense of humor, as well as a thorough scientific knowledge. So it comes as no surprise that she has recently written a series of humor books. She has also authored a collection of folktales from around the world. But readers know Joanna Cole best as the real-life counterpart to everyone's favorite frizzy-haired teacher.

Where to Find Out More About Joanna Cole

Books

Cole, Joanna. *On the Bus with Joanna Cole: A Creative Autobiography.* Portsmouth, N.H.: Heinemann, 1996.

Kovacs, Deborah, and James Preller. *Meet the Authors and Illustrators: 60 Creators of Favorite Children's Books Talk about their Work.* Vol. 1. New York: Scholastic, 1991.

Web Sites

Educational Paperback Association
http://www.edupaperback.org/authorbios/Cole_Joanna.html
To read a biographical sketch and booklist for Joanna Cole

KidsReads.com
http://www.kidsreads.com/authors/au-cole-joanna.asp
To read an autobiographical account of Joanna Cole

Magic School Bus Web Site from Scholastic
http://www.scholastic.com/magicschoolbus/home.htm
For games and an art gallery related to the popular television series

---

It takes about a year for Joanna Cole to write a Magic School Bus book. She spends six months on research and six months on writing.

James Lincoln Collier
Christopher Collier

Born: June 27, 1928 (James)
Born: January 29, 1930 (Christopher)

James Lincoln Collier (pictured below left) and Christopher Collier (pictured below right) are not the only writers in their family. Their father wrote fiction and children's books, an uncle was a novelist, and some of their cousins are journalists. James Lincoln Collier writes historical fiction and nonfiction books for young people with his brother, Christopher. The brothers' best-known books for young people include *My Brother Sam Is Dead, War Comes to Willy Freeman,* and *With Every Drop of Blood.*

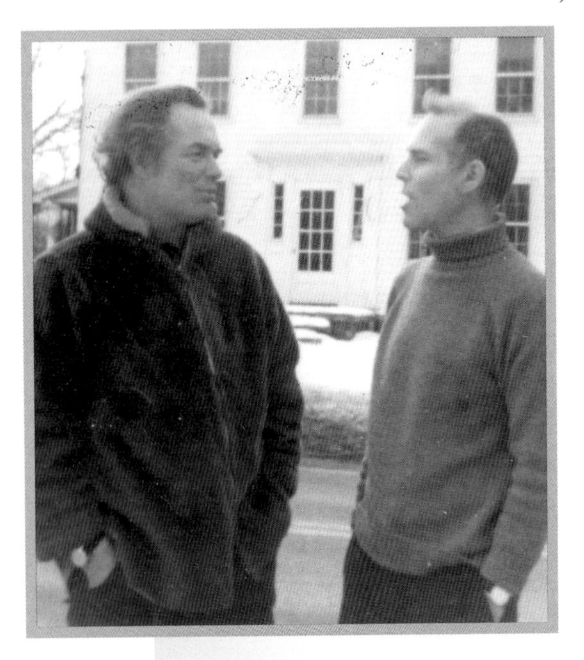

James Lincoln Collier was born on June 27, 1928, in New York City. Because he had so many writers in his family, he knew he wanted to become a writer. After

JAMES LINCOLN COLLIER PLAYS THE TROMBONE FOR A JAZZ BAND IN NEW YORK CITY.

serving in the army for two years, he moved back to New York City. He struggled to find work as a writer and finally took a job as a magazine editor. After about six years, he began to sell his writing to magazines and book publishers. His first nonfiction children's book, *Battleground: The United States Army in World War II,* was published in 1965. He went on to write books about historical events, music, and musicians as well as fiction books for young people.

Christopher Collier was born on January 29, 1930, in New York City. As a young boy, he loved writing. He also became so interested in American history that he went to college and

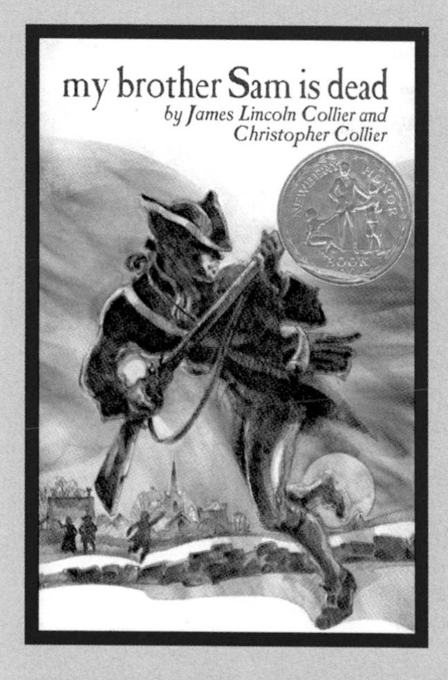

A Selected Bibliography of the Colliers' Work

Wild Boy (James Lincoln Collier only, 2002)
The Changing Face of America, 1945–2000 (2001)
World War Two (2001)
The Rise of the Cities, 1820–1920 (2000)
Andrew Jackson's America, 1824–1850 (1999)
The American Revolution, 1763–1783 (1998)
With Every Drop of Blood (1994)
The Clock (1992)
Who Is Carrie? (1984)
War Comes to Willy Freeman (1983)
Jump Ship to Freedom (1981)
My Brother Sam Is Dead (1974)
Battle Ground: The United States Army in World War II (James Lincoln Collier only, 1965)

The Colliers' Major Literary Awards

1975 Newbery Honor Book
My Brother Sam Is Dead

studied that subject. He is especially interested in the Revolutionary War (1775–1783). Christopher has worked as a history teacher and professor for many years. He has also written about historical events for adults. He did not write for children until he suggested to his brother, James, that they work together on a children's book.

"I am very leery of the term 'artist.' I think of myself as a professional, a craftsman, and I believe that if there is anything such as art, it is the residue of craft."
—James Lincoln Collier

In 1974, the Collier brothers published their first book—*My Brother Sam Is Dead.* They went on to write several other historical fiction books. Because Christopher studies the Revolutionary War as a historian, most of their books are set during the war. The brothers have also written more than twenty nonfiction books for a series called Drama of American History.

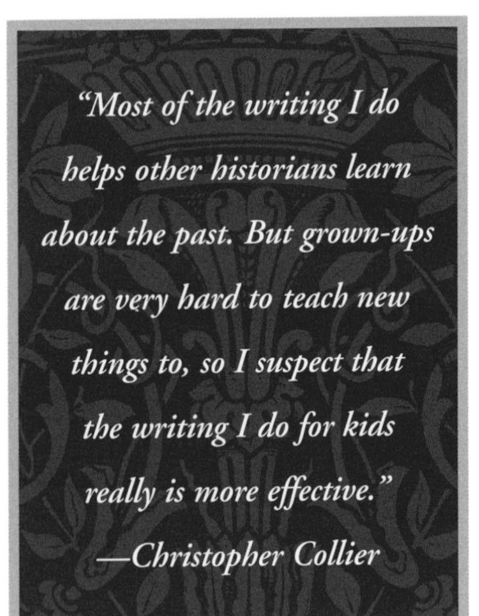

The Collier brothers divide the tasks when they write a book together. First, Christopher thinks of an idea for a book. Then he researches the related details and information. He makes

Christopher Collier was nominated for a Pulitzer Prize in 1971 for a book for adults, *Roger Sherman's Connecticut; Yankee Politics and the American Revolution.*

sure that the facts used in the books are accurate. Using Christopher's research, James writes the story and creates the book's characters. Along with telling an interesting story, the Collier brothers also want to help readers learn about history.

James Lincoln Collier lives in New York and continues to write fiction and nonfiction books for young people. Christopher Collier, now a professor of history, lives in Connecticut. The brothers continue to write books together.

WHERE TO FIND OUT MORE ABOUT JAMES LINCOLN COLLIER AND CHRISTOPHER COLLIER

BOOKS

Collier, Laurie, and Joyce Nakamura, eds. *Major Authors and Illustrators for Children and Young Adults.* Detroit: Gale Research, 1993.

Sutherland, Zena. *Children & Books.* 9th ed. New York: Addison Wesley Longman, 1997.

WEB SITES

EDUCATIONAL PAPERBACK ASSOCIATION
http://www.edupaperback.org/authorbios/Collier_JamesLincoln.html
To read an autobiographical sketch and booklist for James Lincoln Collier

EDUCATIONAL PAPERBACK ASSOCIATION
http://www.edupaperback.org/authorbios/Collier_Christopher.html
To read an autobiographical sketch and booklist for Christopher Collier

---

CHRISTOPHER COLLIER BECAME INTERESTED IN WRITING BOOKS FOR CHILDREN BECAUSE MOST OF THE HISTORY BOOKS HE READ WERE NOT VERY INTERESTING. HE WANTED TO MAKE HISTORY COME ALIVE FOR YOUNG PEOPLE.

Barbara Cooney

Born: August 6, 1917
Died: March 10, 2000

It's hard to know where to begin when writing about an author and artist like Barbara Cooney. Cooney was born on August 6, 1917, and died on March 10, 2000. She wrote and illustrated more than one hundred children's books over a gloriously productive sixty-year career.

Barbara Cooney was born in Brooklyn, New York. Her family moved when she was just two weeks old. Barbara lived in Long Island during the school year and spent the summers in Maine. Barbara and her three brothers loved Maine best.

Young Barbara always knew she would be an artist of some sort. It was in her blood—her great-grandfather, her grandmother, and her

Barbara Cooney had a twin brother.

mother were all artists. As a child, she was allowed to use her mother's art supplies—as long as she kept the brushes clean!

Barbara Cooney studied art and art history at Smith College in Northampton, Massachusetts. Then she packed up her portfolio of artwork and went to New York City to see if she could make a career for herself in children's books. She could! In 1940, she illustrated *Åke and His World,* written by the Swedish poet Bertil Malmberg. The next year she wrote and illustrated her own *King of Wreck Island.*

"I was no more talented than any other child. I started out ruining the wallpaper with crayons, like everybody else, and making eggs with arms and legs."

Barbara Cooney's career as a children's book author and illustrator was interrupted by World War II (1939–1945). In 1942, she joined the Women's Army Corps. Later that same year, she married Guy Murchie. They had two children—Gretel and Barnaby. Barbara and Guy divorced in 1947. Two years later, Cooney married a doctor named C. Talbot Porter. They had two children, Talbot Jr. and Phoebe.

By this time, Barbara Cooney was writing and illustrating several books a year. Although Cooney always said that her first love was color, she did many of her earliest books in black and white.

Whether she was drawing in black and white or in color, however,

BARBARA COONEY LOVED MAINE—AND MAINE LOVED BARBARA. IN 1996, GOVERNMENT OFFICIALS NAMED BARBARA COONEY AN OFFICIAL STATE TREASURE!

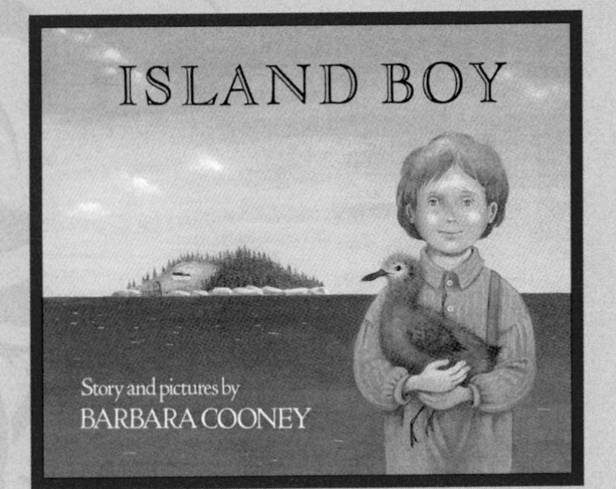

A Selected Bibliography of Cooney's Work

Basket Moon (1999) (Illustrations only)
Eleanor (1996)
Only Opal: The Diary of a Young Girl (Illustrations only, 1994)
Animal Folk Songs for Children: Traditional American Songs (Illustrations only, 1993)
Emily (Illustrations only, 1992)
Letting Swift River Go (Illustrations only, 1992)
Roxaboxen (Illustrations only, 1991)
Hattie and the Wild Waves: A Story from Brooklyn (1990)
Island Boy: Story and Pictures (1988)
The Year of the Perfect Christmas Tree: An Appalachian Story (Illustrations only, 1988)
The Story of Holly and Ivy (Illustrations only, 1985)
Miss Rumphius (1982)
Ox-Cart Man (Illustrations only, 1979)
Seven Little Rabbits (Illustrations only, 1972)
Chanticleer and the Fox (Illustrations only, 1958)
King of Wreck Island (1941)
Åke and His World (Illustrations only, 1940)

Cooney's Major Literary Awards

1989 *Boston Globe–Horn Book* Picture Book Honor Book
Island Boy

1983 American Book Award
Miss Rumphius

1980 Caldecott Medal
Ox-Cart Man

1959 Caldecott Medal
Chanticleer and the Fox

Barbara Cooney always insisted on accuracy and detail. She drew what she knew—plants from her garden, a neighbor's chickens, her own children and their friends. Because Cooney wrote and illustrated folktales, nursery rhymes, and myths from around the world, she traveled extensively to do her research. She wanted to make sure everything—the landscapes, the buildings, the people, and even the light in the air and the color of the sky—was exactly right.

When an editor asked, "How would you like to illustrate a Mother Goose in French?" Cooney didn't hesitate. Packing up her children, she set off for France the following summer. France,

Spain, Switzerland, Ireland, England, Haiti, India, Tunisia, Greece—no country was too far away if Cooney needed to research a book. And she was just as careful about her writing as she was about her drawing!

"'. . . A man's reach should exceed his grasp.' So should a child's. For myself, I will never talk down to—or draw down to—children."

Of all her many books, Barbara Cooney said four were closest to her heart—*Miss Rumphius, Island Boy: Story and Pictures, Hattie and the Wild Waves: A Story from Brooklyn,* and *Eleanor.* These are jewels—but so are the many, many other books she left for readers to treasure.

Where to Find Out More About Barbara Cooney

Books

Silvey, Anita, ed. *Children's Books and Their Creators.* Boston: Houghton Mifflin, 1995.

Sutherland, Zena. *Children & Books.* 9th ed. New York: Addison Wesley Longman, 1997.

Web Sites

CAROL HURST'S CHILDREN'S LITERATURE SITE
http://www.carolhurst.com/newsletters/32dnewsletters.html
To read a biographical sketch of Barbara Cooney and descriptions of her famous books

EDUCATIONAL PAPERBACK ASSOCIATION
http://www.edupaperback.org/authorbios/Cooney_Barbara.html
To read an autobiographical sketch and booklist for Barbara Cooney

COONEY'S ART HAS OFTEN BEEN DESCRIBED AS PRIMITIVE OR FOLK ART. THIS ART STYLE WENT WELL WITH THE KIND OF STORIES SHE USUALLY CHOSE TO WRITE AND ILLUSTRATE—FOLKTALES, NURSERY RHYMES, MYTHS, LEGENDS, AND HISTORICAL BIOGRAPHIES.

Floyd Cooper

Born: January 8, 1956

His warm artwork, often in earth tones of gold and brown, make Floyd Cooper's books special. His illustration technique is called oil wash. In this process, Cooper covers an illustration board with paint and then creates images by erasing them out of the paint.

Floyd Cooper first remembers drawing when he was just three years old. He picked up a piece of Sheetrock at the site of a house his father was building and started scratching out a picture.

Floyd Cooper was born on January 8, 1956, in Tulsa, Oklahoma. He lived there in tenement housing with his family. They didn't have much money, but Floyd's mother inspired her children to be creative and to make something of themselves. Cooper remembers that as a young boy he was always drawing something.

After earning a bachelor of fine arts degree from the University of Oklahoma, Cooper worked in advertising. Then he moved to New York City, hoping to become a famous illustrator. When that didn't work out, he began creating artwork for children's books. And he has never regretted that turn of events!

> *"I feel children's books play a role in counteracting all the violence and other negative images conveyed in the media."*

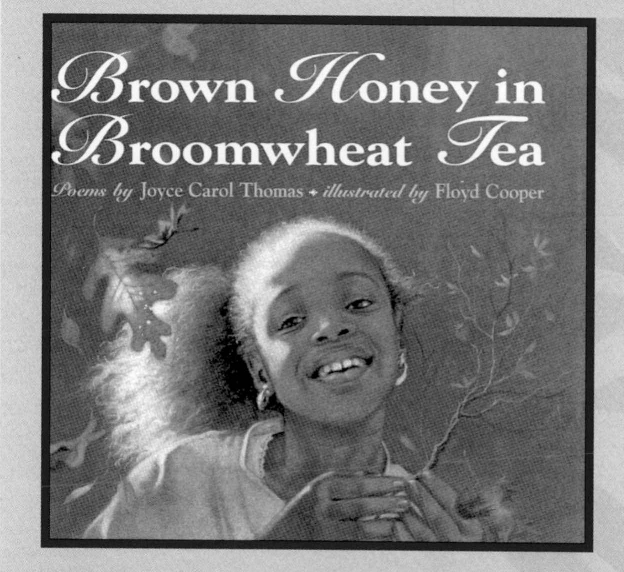

A Selected Bibliography of Cooper's Work

Danitra Brown Leaves Town (Illustrations only, 2002)
Freedom School, Yes! (Illustrations only, 2001)
A Child Is Born (Illustrations only, 2000)
Sweet, Sweet Memory (Illustrations only, 2000)
Granddaddy's Street Songs (Illustrations only, 1999)
Cumbayah (1998)
I Have Heard of a Land (Illustrations only, 1998)
Ma Dear's Aprons (Illustrations only, 1997)
Miz Berlin Walks (Illustrations only, 1997)
Mandela: From the Life of the South African Statesman (1996)
One April Morning: Children Remember the Oklahoma City Bombing (1996)
Satchmo's Blues (Illustrations only, 1996)
Coming Home: From the Life of Langston Hughes (1994)
Jaguarundi (Illustrations only, 1994)
Meet Danitra Brown (Illustrations only, 1994)
Brown Honey in Broomwheat Tea: Poems (Illustrations only, 1993)
Reflections of a Black Cowboy (Illustrations only, 1991)
Grandpa's Face (Illustrations only, 1988)

Cooper's Major Literary Awards

1999 Coretta Scott King Illustrator Honor Book
Have Heard of a Land

1995 Coretta Scott King Illustrator Honor Book
Meet Danitra Brown

1994 Coretta Scott King Illustrator Honor Book
Brown Honey in Broomwheat Tea: Poems

The first book he illustrated was *Grandpa's Face,* written by Eloise Greenfield. Both critics and readers loved his work, so his career as a children's illustrator flourished quickly.

Over the years, Cooper has illustrated many books about African-American culture. His oil creations invite readers to learn about neighborhoods and family relationships, as well as about the lives of famous leaders, writers, and musicians.

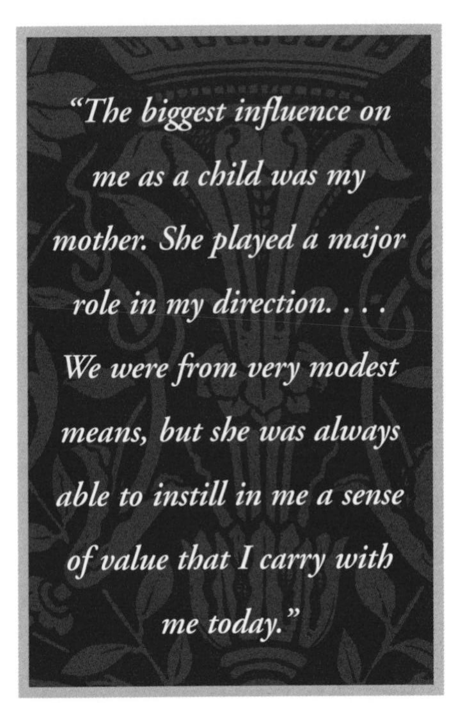

Floyd Cooper has written some of the books he illustrated. One example is *Coming Home: From the Life of Langston Hughes,* a biography of the famous Arican-American poet. He has written and illustrated *Mandela: From the Life of the South African Statesman,* a biography of this courageous South African leader. He has also written *Cumbayah,* a look at a song that people of all ages love to sing around campfires.

One of Cooper's favorite projects was illustrating *Satchmo's Blues,* a book written by Alan Schroeder about jazz musician Louis Armstrong.

In addition to making a living in advertising, Cooper worked for a time as a greeting-card designer for Hallmark.

He has also illustrated collections of poems, a book about Japanese culture, and *One April Morning: Children Remember the Oklahoma City Bombing,* a book about the 1995 attack on a federal office building.

Floyd Cooper lives with his wife and children in New Jersey. He enjoys speaking with young readers and talking about his art.

Where to Find Out More About Floyd Cooper

Books

Holtze, Sally Holmes, ed.
Seventh Book of Junior Authors & Illustrators.
New York: H. W. Wilson Company, 1996.

Something about the Author.
Vol. 96. Detroit: Gale Research, 1998.

Web Sites

Houghton Mifflin: Meet the Author/Illustrator
http://www.eduplace.com/kids/hmr/mtai/fcooper.html
To read a biographical sketch and booklist for Floyd Cooper

Cooper is a fan of all kinds of music, including jazz and the blues, but he says he has "two left ears."

Susan Cooper

Born: May 23, 1935

When Susan Cooper was ten years old, she wrote three puppet plays (the puppeteer was the boy next door). She also wrote a weekly newspaper with her piano teacher's son. And she wrote, illustrated, and sewed together her first book. "My uncle found it in a drawer and came and told me that he liked it, and I was so appalled that somebody had read it that I burst into tears and tore it up," she says.

Susan Cooper was born in Buckinghamshire, England, on May 23, 1935. History was all around her. From her bedroom window, she could see Windsor Castle. An Iron Age fort and part of a road built by the Romans long ago were not far from her home.

Cooper attended Oxford University and was the first woman to edit the university's student newspaper. After graduating, she worked

---

When Susan Cooper went to work for the *Sunday Times* newspaper, her boss was Ian Fleming, the creator of the fictional secret agent James Bond.

for the *Sunday Times* in London.

In her spare time, she wrote a science-fiction novel for adults, *Mandrake,* published in 1964. She heard about a contest for a children's book and wrote *Over Sea, Under Stone.* It started as a simple adventure—until she found herself creating Merriman Lyon, a mysterious character who turns out to be Merlin, the wizard of the legends of King Arthur.

"Read, read, read, anything and everything, prose and poetry and drama. Preferably good stuff, so that its rhythms will echo through your head ever afterwards, even when you aren't aware of them."

Over Sea, Under Stone is the first of the Dark Is Rising series—five stories filled with adventure, a battle between good and evil, and characters based on Arthurian legend. At that time, however, Cooper had no idea that she had started a series. It was eight years before the second book was published. In the meantime, Cooper fell in love with a professor at Massachusetts Institute of Technology and moved to the United States to marry him. She raised his three children and had two of her own. She also wrote articles for a British newspaper, and wrote a novel, *Dawn of Fear,* about a child who lives through the bombing of London in World War II (1939–1945), as Cooper had.

In time, Cooper became homesick for England. One day, while skiing, she had an idea: She would write four interlocking books about

COOPER'S BEST-KNOWN WORK FOR ADULTS ISN'T A BOOK BUT A PLAY, *FOXFIRE,* WHICH RAN FOR SEVEN MONTHS ON BROADWAY. HER COAUTHOR, AND THE STAR OF THE PLAY, WAS ACTOR HUME CRONYN, TO WHOM SHE IS NOW MARRIED.

the characters and situations she had created for *Over Sea, Under Stone*—four books about England. Over the next few years, she wrote *The Dark Is Rising, Greenwitch, The Grey King,* and *Silver on the Tree.* The stories were set in the towns and villages she knew as a child and described legendary figures such as Merlin and King Arthur as well as invented characters, such as Bran, Arthur's son.

Then Susan Cooper turned to other projects. She wrote stories for younger readers, including *The Selkie Girl.* She wrote about the humorous side of legend in her books about the Boggart, a mischievous spirit who lives in a Scottish castle. She also wrote television movies

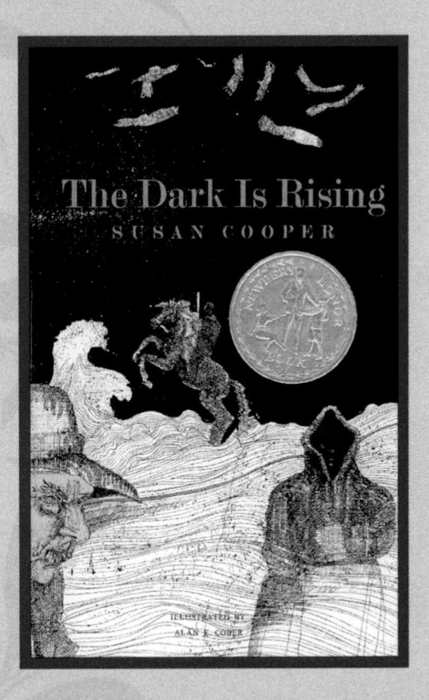

A Selected Bibliography of Cooper's Work

Frog (2002)
Green Boy (2002)
King of Shadows (1999)
The Boggart and the Monster (1997)
Danny and the Kings (1993)
The Boggart (1993)
Matthew's Dragon (1991)
Tam Lin (1991)
The Selkie Girl (1986)
Seaward (1983)
The Silver Cow: A Welsh Tale (1983)
Jethro and the Jumbie (1979)
Silver on the Tree (1977)
The Grey King (1975)
Greenwitch (1974)
The Dark Is Rising (1973)
Dawn of Fear (1970)
Over Sea, Under Stone (1965)

Cooper's Major Literary Awards

2000 *Boston Globe–Horn Book* Fiction Honor Book
King of Shadows

1976 Newbery Medal
The Grey King

1974 Newbery Honor Book
1973 *Boston Globe–Horn Book* Fiction Award
The Dark Is Rising

and several plays. It wasn't until 1999 that she returned to the young adult audience, with *King of Shadows,* the story of a boy actor in 1999 who is transported to 1599, where he gets to work with William Shakespeare.

"At the back of every writer's head there's a small locked room, where the imagination lives. The room has a door with no handle; you can't open it. But once in a great while, for no apparent reason, the door swings open and an idea pops out."

Susan Cooper lives in Connecticut with actor Hume Cronyn. The two married in 1996.

Where to Find Out More About Susan Cooper

Books

Rockman, Connie C., ed. *Eighth Book of Junior Authors and Illustrators.* New York: H. W. Wilson Company, 2000.

Sutherland, Zena. *Children & Books.* 9th ed. New York: Addison Wesley Longman, 1997.

Web Sites

THE AUTHOR: SUSAN COOPER
http://hosted.ukoln.ac.uk/stories/stories/cooper/interview.htm
To read an interview with Susan Cooper

KIDSREADS.COM
http://www.kidsreads.com/authors/au-cooper-susan.asp
To read an autobiographical sketch by Susan Cooper

When Susan Cooper first wrote *Over Sea, Under Stone,* twenty publishers rejected the story.

Lucy Cousins

Born: February 10, 1964

Early in her career, writer and illustrator Lucy Cousins brought some of her work to Wendy Boase, a children's book editor. "I had never seen anything so original," says Boase. "There was nothing quite like her work." Cousins uses thick lines and bold colors to make very simple pictures. Her most famous character is Maisy the mouse. In 1990, the first Maisy book was published. The bright little mouse was an instant hit with tiny children. Babies and toddlers also love lifting the flaps and pulling the tabs in many of Cousins's books.

Today, Maisy is one of the most popular characters among

Maisy's head is never shown from the front. It is always seen in a side view, even on television shows.

very young children. More than 9 million Maisy books have been sold. They have been translated into twenty-one languages. Maisy even has her own television show.

Lucy Cousins was born in Reading, England, on February 10, 1964. She attended Canterbury Art College and Brighton Polytechnic. She then studied graphic design at the Royal College of Art.

Cousins had always loved the art in children's books. She would often go to bookstores to browse through the children's books. Finally, she decided to try making one herself. For her art-school graduation project, she made *Portly's Hat,* a book about a penguin.

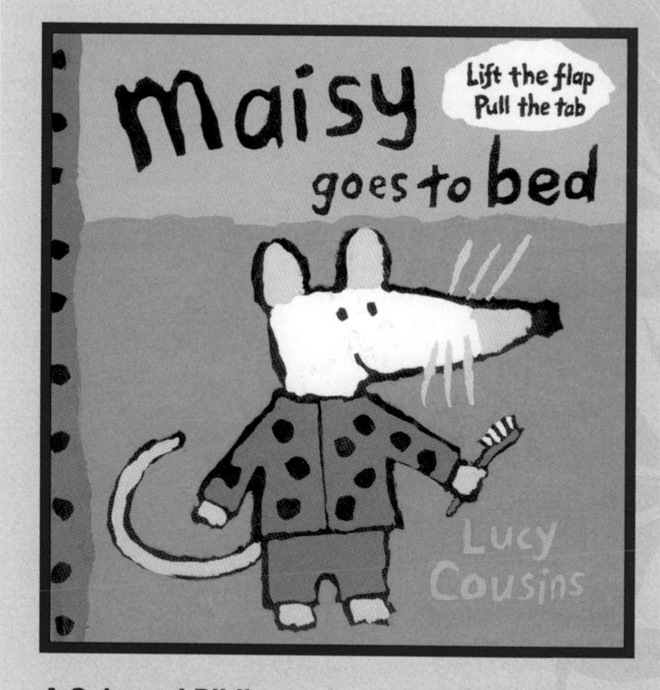

A Selected Bibliography of Cousins's Work

Jazzy in the Jungle (2002)
Doctor Maisy (2001)
Maisy's Favorite Animals (2001)
Maisy Drives the Bus (2000)
Maisy Dresses Up (1999)
Happy Birthday, Maisy (1998)
Count with Maisy (1997)
Za-Za's Baby Brother (1995)
Noah's Ark (1993)
The Little Dog Laughed (Illustrations only, 1990)
Maisy Goes Swimming (1990)
Maisy Goes to Bed (1990)
Portly's Hat (1989)

Then she heard about a competition for art students run by Macmillan, a publishing company in England. *Portly's Hat* won second prize! Macmillan soon published the book. The experience gave Cousins the confidence to try to sell more ideas to book publishers.

"I draw by heart. I think of what children would like by going back to my own childlike instincts."

Since then, Lucy Cousins has turned out dozens of bright, simple books for small children. Some are about animals. Others are collections of nursery rhymes. Many are about Maisy. Maisy stories are the stuff of everyday life. She goes to bed. She goes to school. She makes gingerbread.

Maisy the mouse also stars in an award-winning television show. Cousins was very worried about what would happen to her characters and stories when they were turned into cartoons, so she is very involved in the production of the show. She can reject anything she doesn't like.

To date, Maisy has appeared in more than one hundred books and television shows. But Cousins is not worried about running out of ideas anytime soon. "When you live with small children, you realize there are so many little events that can be made into a story—brushing teeth, losing something, going shopping," explains Cousins. So Maisy and her friends will be

"I get more pleasure and inspiration from walking around a primary school than from any art gallery."

MAISY PRODUCTS ARE POPULAR ALL OVER THE WORLD. IN JAPAN ALONE, MORE THAN 300 MAISY PRODUCTS ARE SOLD, INCLUDING BICYCLES, STAPLERS, AND CHOPSTICKS.

around to entertain babies and toddlers for a long time to come.

These days, Lucy Cousins lives in Hampshire, England, with her four young children. They help her test her books. When she made her first cloth books, her daughter Josie was seven months old. "Josie looked at them and chewed on them and did all the right things," Cousins recalls. She knew she was on the right track.

Where to Find Out More About Lucy Cousins

Books

Rockman, Connie C., ed. *Eighth Book of Junior Authors and Illustrators.* New York: H. W. Wilson Company, 2000.

Silvey, Anita, ed. *Children's Books and Their Creators.* Boston: Houghton Mifflin, 1995.

Web Sites

AABRA KADAABRA'S MAGIC WORLD OF CHILDREN'S BOOKS: MAISY
http://www.aabra.com/Maisy.htm
To view a selection of Maisy titles and synopses

MAISY AT NICKJR.COM
www.nickjr.com/kids/html_site/maisy/
To find out more about Maisy's friends

ALTHOUGH MAISY IS AN OUTGOING LITTLE MOUSE, HER CREATOR DOESN'T MUCH LIKE ATTENTION. LUCY COUSINS ALMOST NEVER DOES INTERVIEWS OR BOOK SIGNINGS.

Helen Craig

Born: August 30, 1934

"Most people are in their twenties when they discover what they want to do in life," Helen Craig explains. It took her almost forty years to decide that she wanted to illustrate children's books! Since then, Craig has written and illustrated the popular *The Mouse House ABC, Susie and Alfred in The Night of the Paper Bag Monsters,* and *The Town Mouse and the Country Mouse.* She is best known as the illustrator of the Angelina Ballerina series written by Katharine Holabird.

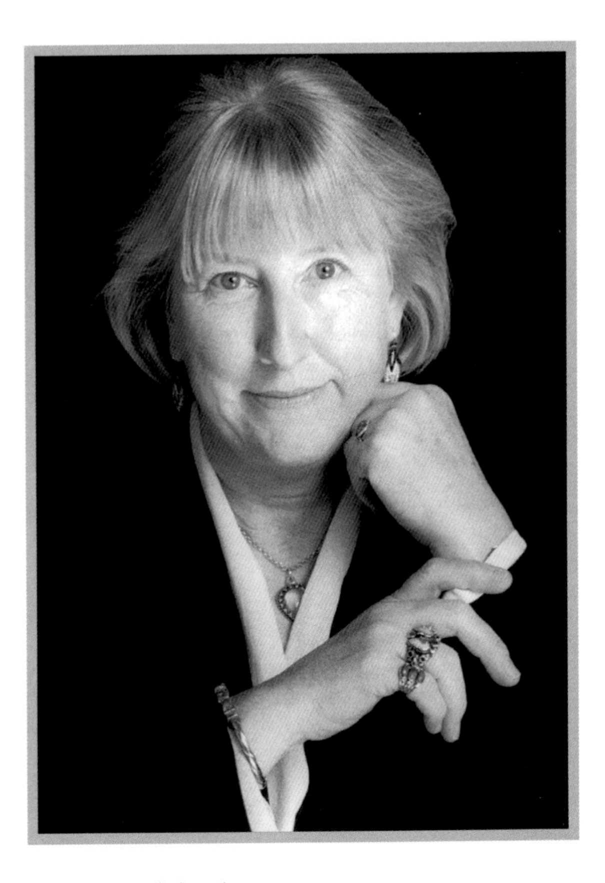

Helen Craig was born on August 30, 1934, in London, England.

Helen Craig has worked as a potter, a sculptor, and a restorer of Chinese wallpaper.

She grew up in a family of artists. Her grandfather was a stage designer for the theater. Her father was an art director for films, and her brother was an illustrator and graphic designer.

"As a child I had been strongly impressed by the books I looked at and read, and can still recall those feelings and try to remember them when working."

"It had always been my ambition that one day I would be a creative artist of some sort," says Craig. But as a teenager, Helen did not think her art was as good as that of other members of her family. So instead of becoming an artist, she went to work with a photographer. She learned how to take pictures and she became a very talented photographer. Several years later, she started her own photography studio.

Craig was hired to take pictures for magazines and advertising. While she was working as a photographer, she continued to draw. She found drawing to be relaxing. She did not show her drawings to anyone, though. She was not sure her work was any good!

Craig's interest in illustrating children's books developed after her son was born in 1965. As she read books to her son, she imagined how exciting it would be to illustrate a book for children herself.

A few years later, Craig showed some of her drawings and a story

---

THREE OF CRAIG'S BOOKS HAVE BEEN CHOSEN FOR THE BRITISH BOOK DESIGN AND PRODUCTION EXHIBITIONS.

she had written to an editor. The work was not published, but she was asked to illustrate a book written by another author. That book, written by Robert Nye, was called *Wishing Gold.* It was published in 1970. Craig went on to illustrate other books written by other authors. *The Mouse House ABC* was the first book she wrote and illustrated. It was published in 1979.

> *"Every illustrator always wants to produce beautiful pictures, but for me the most important element is to make the characters communicate with each other. I hope I manage to do this."*

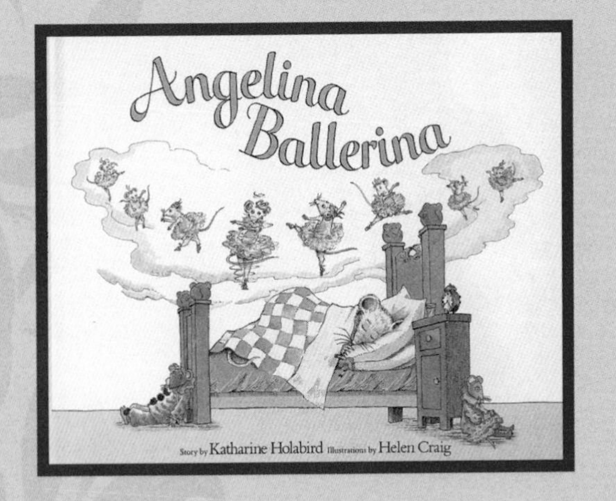

A Selected Bibliography of Craig's Work

Angelina and the Butterfly (Illustrations only, 2002)
Rosy's Visitors (Illustrations only, 2002)
Angelina's Birthday (Illustrations only, 2001)
Angelina's Halloween (Illustrations only, 2000)
Panda's New Toy (Illustrations only, 1999)
Turnover Tuesday (Illustrations only, 1998)
Charlie and Tyler at the Seashore (1995)
Susie and Alfred in The Night of the Paper Bag Monsters (1994)
I See the Moon and the Moon Sees Me—: Helen Craig's Book of Nursery Rhymes (1992)
The Town Mouse and the Country Mouse (1992)
Susie and Alfred in The Knight, the Princess and the Dragon (1987)
Susie and Alfred in A Welcome for Annie (1986)
Angelina Ballerina (Illustrations only, 1983)
The Mouse House ABC (1979)
Wishing Gold (Illustrations only, 1970)

The inspiration for Craig's illustrations comes from a variety of places. She uses memories from her childhood to create many of her illustrations. "Now that I'm an illustrator myself, I try to make my pictures live for the children who look at them, as those pictures did for me when I was a child," Craig notes.

Helen Craig continues to write and illustrate books for children. She lives in Aylesbury, England.

Where to Find Out More About Helen Craig

Books

Rockman, Connie C., ed. *Eighth Book of Junior Authors and Illustrators.* New York: H. W. Wilson Company, 2000.

Silvey, Anita, ed. *Children's Books and Their Creators.* Boston: Houghton Mifflin, 1995.

Web Sites

ANGELINA BALLERINA
http://www.angelinaballerina.com/
To play a ballerina game and make mini-posters

TOONHOUND—ANGELINA BALLERINA
http://www.toonhound.com/angelina.htm
To read an episode list of the television series

HELEN CRAIG DESIGNED AN ANGELINA BALLERINA DOLL THAT WAS BASED ON HER DRAWINGS FOR THE BOOKS.

Sharon Creech

Born: July 29, 1945

In *Walk Two Moons*, thirteen-year-old Salamanca Tree Hiddle searches for her mother, while *The Wanderer's* Sophie, also thirteen, learns about her family on a sailing trip across the ocean. Mary Lou Finney tells about her thirteenth summer in *Absolutely Normal Chaos.* With these teenage characters, Sharon Creech writes stories of love and loss, happiness and heartache.

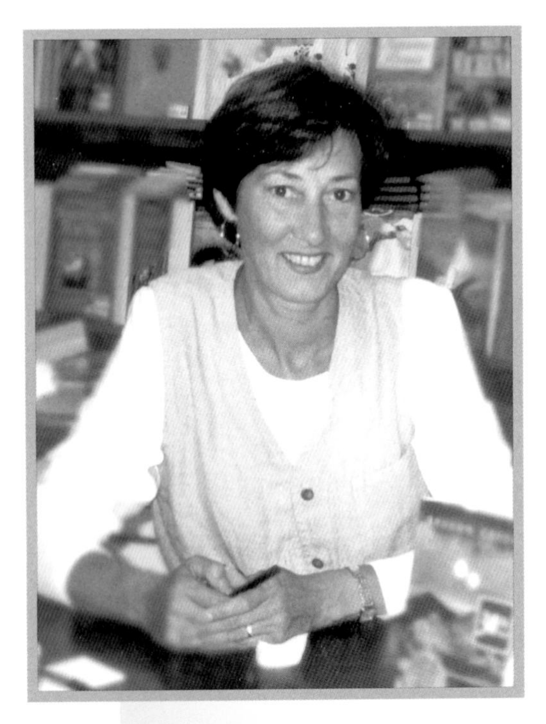

Sharon Creech was born on July 29, 1945, in South Euclid, Ohio, a suburb of Cleveland. She grew up in a large family, in a house full of people who loved to tell stories. As a young woman, Sharon was always drawn to reading and writing, and she collected paper, pens, and books. After high school, she enrolled at Hiram College

Sharon Creech wrote two books under the name Sharon Rigg—*The Recital* and *Nickel Malley.* They were published only in England.

in Ohio, where she earned her bachelor's degree. Then she moved on to George Mason University in Virginia, where she earned her master's degree.

Creech's first jobs after college were working as a researcher for the Federal Theater Project Archives and as an editorial assistant at *Congressional Quarterly,* in Washington, D.C. She found these positions to be terribly boring, though, because they involved facts and

"I don't remember the titles of books I read as a child, but I do remember the experience of reading—of drifting into the pages and living in someone else's world."

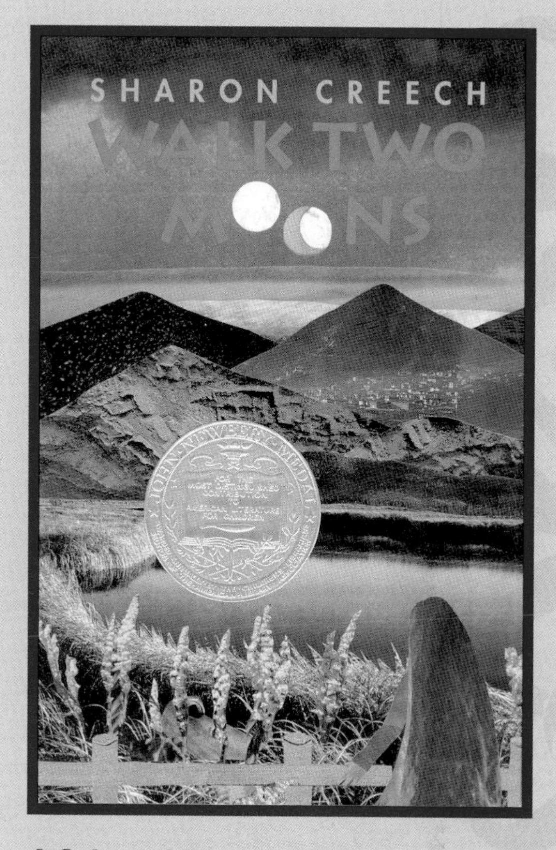

A Selected Bibliography of Creech's Work

A Fine, Fine School (2001)
Love That Dog (2001)
Fishing in the Air (2000)
The Wanderer (2000)
Bloomability (1998)
Chasing Redbird (1997)
Pleasing the Ghost (1996)
Absolutely Normal Chaos (1995)
Walk Two Moons (1994)

Creech's Major Literary Awards

2001 Newbery Honor Book
The Wanderer

1995 Newbery Medal
Walk Two Moons

"I wanted to be many things when I grew up: a painter, an ice skater, a singer, a teacher, and a reporter. . . . I soon learned that I would make a terrible reporter because when I didn't like the facts, I changed them."

numbers rather than thoughts and ideas. In Washington, Creech got married, had two children, and then divorced.

Creech's next move was more exciting. She and her children left the United States and moved to England, where she taught literature at a boarding school. There she met Lyle Rigg, an assistant headmaster, and they were married. They remained in England for a time. Next they were transferred to a boarding school in Switzerland but later returned to England.

Through these adventures, Sharon Creech realized she had much to write about. She published her first book for young readers, *Absolutely Normal Chaos*, in England in 1990, but it was not released in the United States until five years later. In the meantime, she wrote *Walk Two Moons,* the book that made her famous as an author.

Her stories about young people appeal to readers because they deal with real problems in a real way. Creech's characters worry about families and schoolwork as well as about boyfriends and girlfriends. Creech also

---

THE TITLE FOR *WALK TWO MOONS* CAME FROM THIS MESSAGE IN A FORTUNE COOKIE: "DON'T JUDGE A MAN UNTIL YOU'VE WALKED TWO MOONS IN HIS MOCCASINS."

sets her stories in places all over the world—in cities and towns she has lived in and visited.

As much as she enjoyed her time in Europe, Sharon Creech missed the United States. So she and her husband recently moved to New Jersey. She continues to write, and Rigg is the headmaster of a private school. When Creech is not writing, she still enjoys teaching and tutoring, and she loves spending time outdoors and with her grown children.

Where to Find Out More about Sharon Creech

Books

Hedblad, Alan. *Major Authors and Illustrators for Children and Young Adults.* Detroit: Gale Research, 1998.

Holtze, Sally Holmes, ed. *Seventh Book of Junior Authors & Illustrators.* New York: H. W. Wilson Company, 1996.

Web Sites

Educational Paperback Association
http://www.edupaperback.org/authorbios/Creech_Sharon.html
To read an autobiographical sketch by and booklist for Sharon Creech

Sharon Creech's Web Site
http://sharoncreech.com/
To read a brief biography about Sharon Creech and learn more about her books

In addition to her books, Creech wrote the play *The Center of the Universe: Waiting for the Girl,* which was produced in New York City in 1992.

Donald Crews

Born: August 30, 1938

The things that catch Donald Crews's eye are a lot like the things that catch the attention of children. He is interested in dots, motion, and shapes. As an artist, he has a fresh way of looking at the world. Through his bold, solid illustrations, simple things such as a steam train chugging along the tracks come alive.

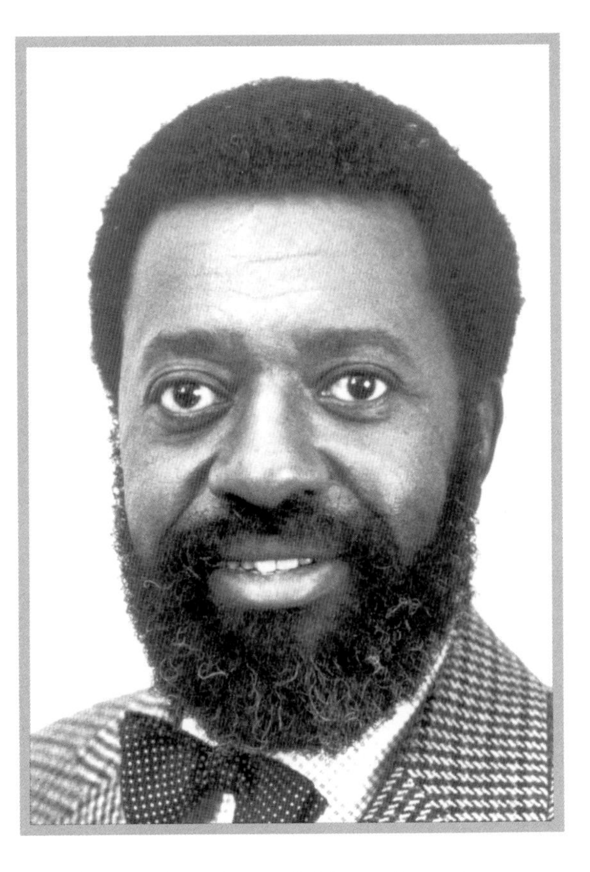

Donald Crews was born on August 30, 1938, in Newark, New Jersey, in a large African-American family. Donald's father was a railroad trackman, responsible for the

DONALD CREWS'S CREATIVE USE OF PHOTOGRAPHS TO ILLUSTRATE CHILDREN'S BOOKS HAS GAINED HIM MUCH PRAISE. IN *CAROUSEL,* FOR EXAMPLE, HE USED A COLLAGE OF PICTURES OF A CAROUSEL TO CREATE THE IMPRESSION OF ITS CIRCULAR MOVEMENT.

stretches of rails that carried the swift-moving steam trains that fascinated his son. His mother was a dressmaker and craftswoman.

Crews attributes his artistic interests to his mother. Her dressmaking tools resembled the tools of the graphic artist. She worked with geometric patterns and chose swaths of cloth for their colors and textures. Donald's brother and two sisters all inherited this creative impulse.

For as long as he can remember, Crews has been sketching. His skill in the visual arts won him a place at an arts high school, where he devoted most of his time to painting, drawing, and photography. After high school, he attended the Cooper Union for the Advancement of Science and Art in New York City.

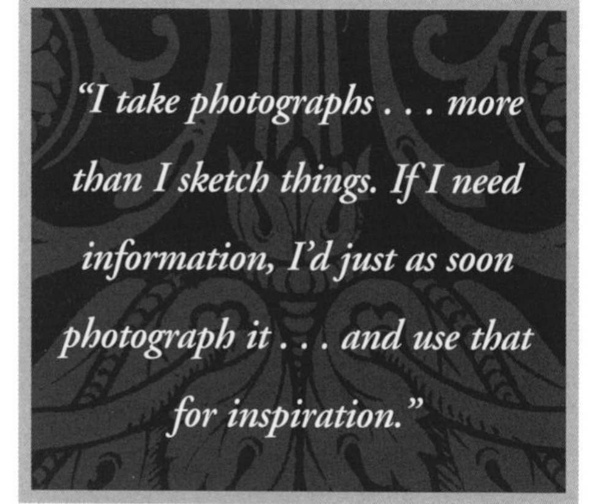

At Cooper Union, Crews met a fellow student—author, artist, and designer Ann Jonas. After working as an assistant art director at *Dance* magazine and a staff designer for a studio in New York City, Donald Crews joined the U.S. Army. Donald married Ann in 1964, while stationed in Germany. They had two daughters, Nina Melissa and Amy Marshanna.

In Germany, Crews wrote and illustrated his first children's book—*We Read: A to Z.* In this book, vivid illustrations introduce the letters of

CREWS'S ABILITY TO EXPRESS AN IDEA CLEARLY IN IMAGES LED HIM TO ILLUSTRATE A SERIES OF MATH AND SCIENCE BOOKS, INCLUDING *FRACTIONS ARE PARTS OF THINGS* AND THE *ABC OF ECOLOGY.*

the alphabet. Crews originally planned to include the project in his portfolio, but in 1967, *We Read: A to Z* was accepted for publication. Crews's powerful pictures hold the very young reader's attention and are ideally suited for those trying to grasp reading basics. The next year, Crews's *Ten Black Dots,* which introduces numbers, was published.

The memory of sitting on his grandparents' porch in Cottondale, Florida, and watch-

> *"It's very heady to be called an author and writer, to know that things you create could be useful."*

A Selected Bibliography of Crews's Work

Cloudy Day/Sunny Day (1999)
Night at the Fair (1997)
More Than One (Illustrations only, 1996)
Sail Away (1995)
Tomorrow's Alphabet (Illustrations only, 1995)
When This Box Is Full (Illustrations only, 1993)
Each Orange Had Eight Slices: A Counting Book (Illustrations only, 1992)
Shortcut (1992)
Bigmama's (1991)
Flying (1986)
Bicycle Race (1985)
School Bus (1984)
Parade (1983)
Carousel (1982)
Harbor (1982)
Light (1981)
Truck (1980)
Blue Sea (Illustrations only, 1979)
Freight Train (1978)
Rain (Illustrations only, 1978)
Eclipse; Darkness in Daytime (Illustrations only, 1973)
ABC of Ecology (Illustrations only, 1972)
Fractions Are Parts of Things (Illustrations only, 1971)
ABC Science Experiments (Illustrations only, 1970)
Ten Black Dots (1968)
We Read: A to Z (1967)

Crews's Major Literary Awards

1981 Caldecott Honor Book
Truck

1979 Caldecott Honor Book
Freight Train

ing the trains go by, inspired Crews's 1978 award-winning *Freight Train.* The experience convinced the author/illustrator that he could create picture books for a living, and so he left his career as a designer.

Today, Donald Crews lives with his wife in New York. As a full-time writer, Crews travels to schools and meets the children, parents, and teachers who read his books in the classroom and at home. He is always surprised by their enthusiasm, which convinces him anew that what he is doing is, after all, important work.

Where to Find Out More About Donald Crews

Books

Holtze, Sally Holmes, ed. *Fifth Book of Junior Authors & Illustrators.* New York: H. W. Wilson Company, 1983.

Kovacs, Deborah, and James Preller. *Meet the Authors and Illustrators: 60 Creators of Favorite Children's Books Talk about Their Work.* Vol. 1. New York: Scholastic, 1991.

Web Sites

STUDIO VIEWS—DONALD CREWS
http://www.hbook.com/studio_crews.shtml
To read an excerpt from the *Horn Book* about why Crews likes to draw with pencils

UNIVERSITY OF OMAHA: BIOGRAPHY OF DONALD CREWS
http://www.unomaha.edu/~unochlit/Crews.html
To read a short biography of Donald Crews, synopses of some of his books, and a booklist

---

IN 1979 CREWS'S *FREIGHT TRAIN* WAS EXHIBITED IN THE AMERICAN INSTITUTE OF GRAPHIC ARTS CHILDREN'S BOOK SHOW.

Christopher Paul Curtis

Born: May 10, 1954

Christopher Paul Curtis was not sure he could be a successful writer. "I give a lot of the credit for my writing career to my wife," Curtis notes. "She had more faith in my ability to write than I did." His first book was published in 1995. *The Watsons Go to Birmingham—1963* is a novel about an African-American family who travel South for a vacation during the Civil Rights era. In 1999, Curtis published his next book, *Bud, Not Buddy,* about a motherless boy who takes to the road in 1936.

Christopher Paul Curtis was born on May 10, 1954, in Flint, Michigan. He grew up and went to school there. His parents had strict rules that Christopher was expected to obey. When he finished high school, he wanted to go to college,

Curtis studied political science in college and helped run the campaign for a U.S. Congressional candidate.

but he had to get a job and earn money instead.

Christopher's father worked at an automotive-assembly plant in Flint. Curtis took a job fitting doors on the cars at the plant. He held that job for more than thirteen years, working on his writing when he could.

After several years, Curtis began attending the University of Michigan at night. As a student, he won a prize for his writing. His wife encouraged him to pursue a career as a writer. They decided that he

"I often tell students that the best practice for writing is to do it at every opportunity."

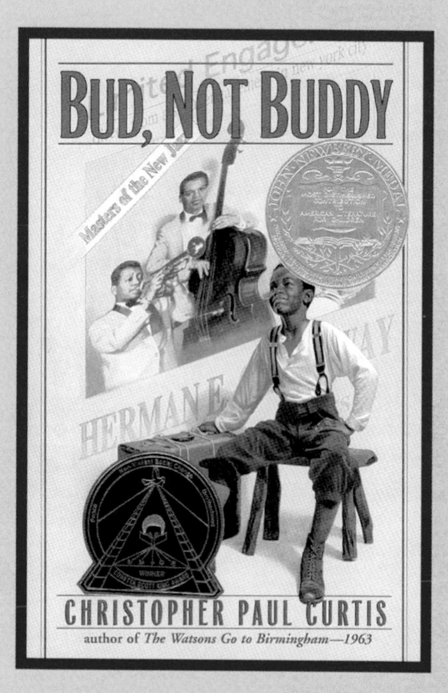

A Selected Bibliography of Curtis's Work

Bud, Not Buddy (1999)

The Watsons Go to Birmingham–1963 (1995)

Curtis's Major Literary Awards

2000 Coretta Scott King Author Award
2000 Newbery Medal
Bud, Not Buddy

1996 Coretta Scott King Author Honor Book
1996 Newbery Honor Book
The Watsons Go to Birmingham–1963

> *"I used to write during breaks because it took me away from being in the factory. I didn't like being there so I would sit down and write. It was much like reading, it would take me away from where I was."*

would quit his job at the plant to concentrate on his writing. He completed his college degree in 1996.

Every day Curtis worked at a table in the children's section of the local library. He wrote on sheets of paper. His son took his father's words and typed them into a computer. When the book was finished, Curtis entered it into a national writing contest. Although the book did not win the contest, an editor of a publishing company liked the manuscript enough to publish it! *The Watsons Go to Birmingham—1963* went on to win several awards.

Curtis has a strong connection to the city where he grew up. All his books are set in Flint. He has many memories from growing up there and uses the city's history in his books. Another important influence in his writing was his job at the automobile plant. "My job was hanging doors, and I still have nightmares about the numbing repetitiveness of the work, but I believe it helped me become a writer," he explains. "It helped me develop the discipline to write daily."

Curtis now lives with his family in Windsor, Ontario, Canada. He

---

ACTOR WHOOPI GOLDBERG PURCHASED THE RIGHTS TO ADAPT *THE WATSONS GO TO BIRMINGHAM—1963* INTO A MOTION PICTURE.

continues to write books for young adults. He also travels and visits schools to talk to young people about his writing. "Many times young people feel that writing is, or should be, the result of a consultation with some mysterious, hard-to-find muse," says Curtis. "I don't think so. I think in many ways writing is much like learning a second language or playing a sport or mastering a musical instrument: the more you do it, the better you become at it."

Where to Find Out More About Christopher Paul Curtis

Books

Rockman, Connie C., ed. *Eighth Book of Junior Authors and Illustrators.* New York: H. W. Wilson Company, 2000.

Something about the Author. Vol. 93. Detroit: Gale Research, 1997.

Web Sites

Educational Paperback Association
http://www.edupaperback.org/authorbios/Curtis_ChristopherPaul.html
To read an autobiographical sketch of Christopher Paul Curtis

Random House Authors/Illustrators
http://www.randomhouse.com/teachers/authors/curt.html
To read a biographical sketch of Christopher Paul Curtis

Both of Curtis's grandfathers had interesting jobs. One of his grandfathers was a pitcher in the Negro baseball league and the other was the leader of a band.

Karen Cushman

Born: October 4, 1941

Karen Cushman was fifty-three years old when she published her first book. It wasn't that she hadn't been interested in writing before that, however. Cushman spent much of her childhood reading her way through the town library and writing stories, plays, poems, and new plots for Elvis Presley movies. But growing up in a working-class suburb of Chicago, Illinois, in the 1940s, she didn't realize that she could make a career out of writing.

Karen Cushman was born in Chicago on October 4, 1941. Her family moved to Tarzana, California, when she was eleven. Karen did well in school and won a scholarship to any college of her choice. She chose Stanford University, where she studied English and Greek, thinking she

CUSHMAN'S WRITING AS A TEENAGER INCLUDED "JINGLE BAGELS," A CHRISTMAS/HANUKKAH PLAY IN WHICH SANTA CLAUS GOES DOWN THE WRONG CHIMNEY.

might become an archaeologist. Instead, she got a job working for the phone company, the first of a series of boring jobs. She quit them all.

She met her husband, Philip, when he was studying to be a rabbi. They moved to Oregon, where, Karen says, "I wove and made blackberry jam and had a daughter, Leah." Her daughter was born in 1973.

After a few years, the Cushmans moved back to California. Karen got a master's degree in counseling and another in museum studies—a subject she taught for many years thereafter.

"I like writing because it's something I can do at home barefoot; because I can lie on my bed and read and call it work; because I am always making up stories in my head anyway and I might as well make a living from them."

Leah grew up and grew out of the children's books she and her mother had read together, but Karen Cushman remained interested. She would tell her husband about ideas for books of her own. One day he replied, "Don't tell me about it. Write it."

So Cushman did just that. She wrote seven pages about a girl in the Middle Ages who thinks she is going to be forced to marry a rich landowner. Then came the hard part—finding out how people actually lived in the thirteenth century. She needed to know about their food and their table manners, their beliefs and their superstitions, how they cured a

---

When Cushman was writing her first novel, many people tried to discourage her. They told her that historical fiction wouldn't sell and that boys wouldn't read a story about girls.

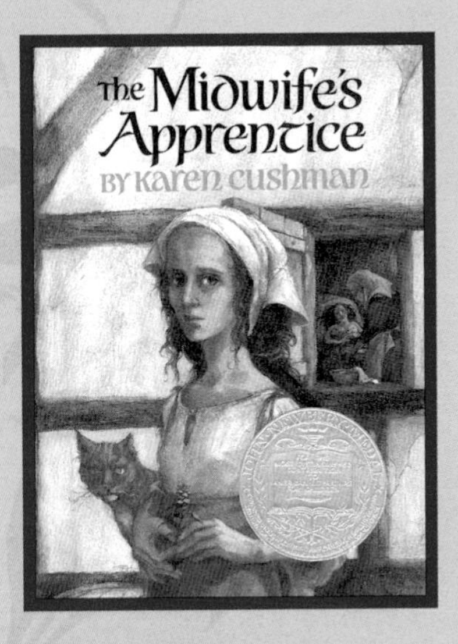

A Selected Bibliography of Cushman's Work

Matilda Bone (2000)
The Ballad of Lucy Whipple (1996)
The Midwife's Apprentice (1995)
Catherine, Called Birdy (1994)

Cushman's Major Literary Awards

1996 Newbery Medal
The Midwife's Apprentice

1995 Newbery Honor Book
Catherine, Called Birdy

toothache, how they took a bath. She researched and she read. Then she wrote. Three years later, her book was finished—*Catherine, Called Birdy.* The novel was very popular and received several awards, including the Newbery Honor.

Cushman's second book was also set in the Middle Ages, so it took only six months to write. *The Midwife's Apprentice* tells the story of an "unwashed, unnourished, unloved, and unlovely" girl named Brat, who learns how to deliver babies and discovers much about herself at

"I used to imagine I was the only child ever kidnapped from gypsies and sold to regular people."

the same time. Published in 1995, it won the Newbery Medal.

For her third book, Cushman switched to the nineteenth century. She read that 90 percent of the people who took part in the California Gold Rush in 1849 were men. She went back to the library to do the research, and in 1996 published *The Ballad of Lucy Whipple,* the story of a twelve-year-old girl "who didn't want any part of the Gold Rush but had no choice." Another medieval book, *Matilda Bone,* set in the world of medicine, followed in 2000.

"I've always been a late bloomer," Cushman said in an interview. "But I always eventually bloom. Here I am making a new career late in life and having a wonderful time."

Where to Find Out More about Karen Cushman

Books

Something about the Author. Vol. 89. Detroit: Gale Research, 1997.

Web Sites

Author Spotlight
http://www.eduplace.com/rdg/author/cushman/index.html
To read a transcript of an interview with Karen Cushman

Educational Paperback Association
http://www.edupaperback.org/authorbios/Cushman_Karen.html
To read an autobiographical sketch of Karen Cushman

When *Catherine, Called Birdy* was named a Newbery Honor Book, Cushman was so new to children's literature that she had to find out what the Newbery Medal was before she realized how well she had done.

Roald Dahl

Born: September 13, 1916
Died: November 23, 1990

Roald Dahl never intended to be a writer. He wanted to visit faraway countries and have exciting adventures. It was almost by accident that his first story was published. After that, he wrote many books, plays, and movie screenplays for adults and children. He is best known for the children's books *James and the Giant Peach: A Children's Story; Charlie and the Chocolate Factory; The Magic Finger; Matilda;* and *Danny, the Champion of the World.*

Roald Dahl was born on September 13, 1916, in Llandaff, Wales. He had five sisters and one brother. Sadly, his father died when Roald was four years old.

Roald was an energetic child who loved getting into mischief. He attended an all-boys boarding school where discipline was very strict.

Dahl invented a new word for his book *The Gremlins*. The word was "gremlin"!

Roald was often beaten when he got into trouble. This cruelty became a part of the stories he wrote as an adult.

After high school, Roald's mother wanted him to attend Oxford University, a famous school in England. Dahl had no interest in going to Oxford. He wanted a job with a company that would send him to faraway places. Shell Oil hired Dahl and sent him to Tanzania.

In 1939, Dahl became a fighter pilot for Great Britain in World War II (1939–1945). Flying over Egypt, his plane was hit by machine-gun fire and crashed. He was badly injured and ultimately had to stop flying.

Then Dahl was transferred

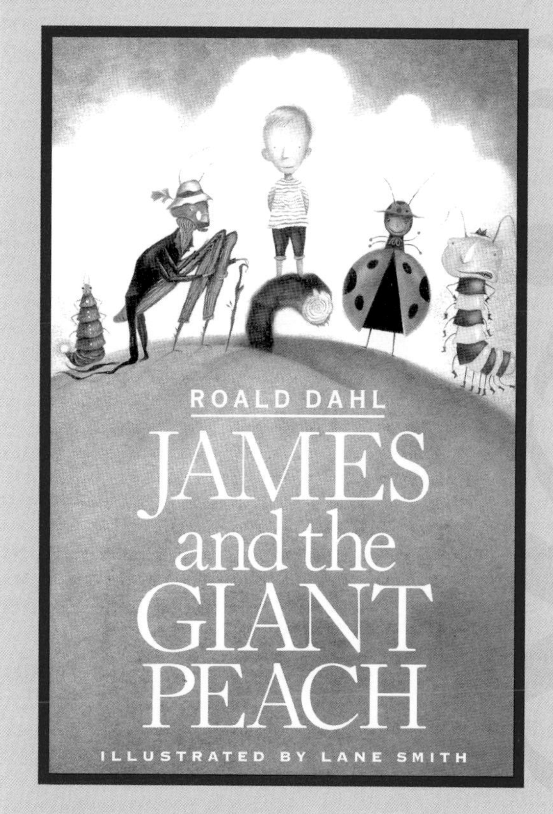

A Selected Bibliography of Dahl's Work

Matilda (1988)
Boy: Tales of Childhood (1984)
The Witches (1983)
The BFG (1982)
The Twits (1980)
The Enormous Crocodile (1978)
The Wonderful Story of Henry Sugar and Six More (1977)
Danny, the Champion of the World (1975)
Charlie and the Great Glass Elevator (1972)
Fantastic Mr. Fox (1970)
Charlie and the Chocolate Factory (1964)
James and the Giant Peach: A Children's Story (1961)
The Gremlins (1943)

Dahl's Major Literary Awards

1985 *Boston Globe–Horn Book* Nonfiction Honor Book
Boy: Tales of Childhood

"If you think a child is getting bored, you must think up something that jolts it back. Something that tickles. You have to know what children like."

to Washington, D.C. There the *Saturday Evening Post* magazine asked him to write a story about being a fighter pilot. It earned him $1,000 and was the beginning of Dahl's writing career. "But becoming a writer was pure fluke," remembered Dahl. "Without being asked to, I doubt if I'd ever have thought of it."

Dahl wrote his first children's story, *The Gremlins,* in 1943. It was a success, and Dahl became a full-time writer. During the next seventeen years, he wrote many short stories for adults. During this time, he married actor Patricia O'Neal. They had one son and four daughters (one of whom died in childhood).

At home, Roald Dahl began making up stories for his children at bedtime. Soon, he was writing these stories for publication. In 1961, he published a children's book about the adventures of a young orphan who is forced to live with his two wicked aunts. It was called *James and the Giant Peach: A Children's Story.*

From that time on, Dahl focused on writing for children. The cruelty he remembered from his own childhood was a common theme in his stories. His stories were often fantasies and adventures told with

DAHL WROTE MOST OF HIS CHILDREN'S BOOKS IN A TINY HUT IN AN ORCHARD AT HIS HOME IN BUCKINGHAMSHIRE, ENGLAND.

humor and understanding. Over the years, Dahl's books have sold millions of copies.

After Dahl and O'Neal divorced in 1983, Dahl remarried. Roald Dahl continued writing until his death on November 23, 1990, in Oxford, England. He was seventy-four.

"The writer for children must be a jokey sort of a fellow. . . . [H]e must like simple tricks and jokes and riddles and other childish things."

Where to Find Out More about Roald Dahl

Books

Dahl, Roald. *Going Solo.* New York: Puffin Books, 1999.

Gaines, Ann Graham. *Roald Dahl.* Bear, Del.: Mitchell Lane Publishers, 2002.

Shavick, Andrea. *Roald Dahl: The Champion Storyteller.* New York: Oxford University Press, 1998.

Shields, Charles J. *Roald Dahl.* Broomall, Pa.: Chelsea House Publishers, 2002.

Web Sites

Educational Paperback Association
http://www.edupaperback.org/authorbios/Dahl_Roald.html
To read an autobiographical sketch and booklist for Roald Dahl

Official Roald Dahl Web Site
http://www.roalddahl.com/getplugin/image.htm
To read about Roald Dahl, his books, and characters

Roald Dahl Fans
http://www.roalddahlfans.com/
To read a biographical sketch, timeline, and booklist for Roald Dahl

---

Movies based on Dahl's books include *James and the Giant Peach, Willy Wonka and the Chocolate Factory,* and *Matilda.*

Paula Danziger

Born: August 18, 1944

Paula Danziger knew from the time she was seven years old that she wanted to be a writer. Paula was born in Washington, D.C., on August 18, 1944. As a child, she loved reading books, sharing her sense of humor, and telling stories. But Paula's childhood wasn't easy, and she didn't do very well in school. "All writers write from deep experience," says Danziger. "For me, that is childhood. From it flows feelings of vulnerability, compassion, and strength."

After high school, Danziger went to Montclair State College in New Jersey and studied to become a teacher. While she was at college, she met writer and poet John Ciardi. She became friends with him and his family. He taught her about language and encouraged her studies. After graduating in 1967, Danziger taught English in junior high school.

IN HIGH SCHOOL, PAULA DANZIGER WROTE FOR NEWSPAPERS AT SCHOOL AND IN HER COMMUNITY.

"When I was a child, I always looked at strangers and made up stories about them—who they were, what their lives were like. Back then I was called a daydreamer. Now I am called a writer."

While she was earning a master's degree in reading, Danziger was in two car accidents. As she struggled to recover, she decided to start writing a novel. It was about a thirteen-year-old girl named Marcy Lewis who was also struggling in life. Through Marcy's experiences, Danziger was able to deal with the challenges in her own recovery. *The Cat Ate My Gymsuit was* an immediate success when it was published in 1974.

Paula Danziger's career as a writer had begun. She returned briefly to teaching, but she continued to write. Danziger writes about the typical problems of young people. At the same time, she helps readers find humor in the situations that frustrate them. Danziger says, "Like a good friend, a book can help you see things a little more clearly, help you blow off steam, get you laughing, let you cry."

"Here I am a full-time writer, a 'grown-up' who chooses to write about kids. I've made this choice because I think that kids and adults share a lot of the same feelings and thoughts—that we have to go through a lot of similar situations."

Danziger's extremely popular books include the

DANZIGER GETS HER IDEAS FROM THE EXPERIENCES OF REAL KIDS. HER FIRST AMBER BROWN BOOK WAS THE RESULT OF HER NIECE'S BEST FRIEND MOVING AWAY.

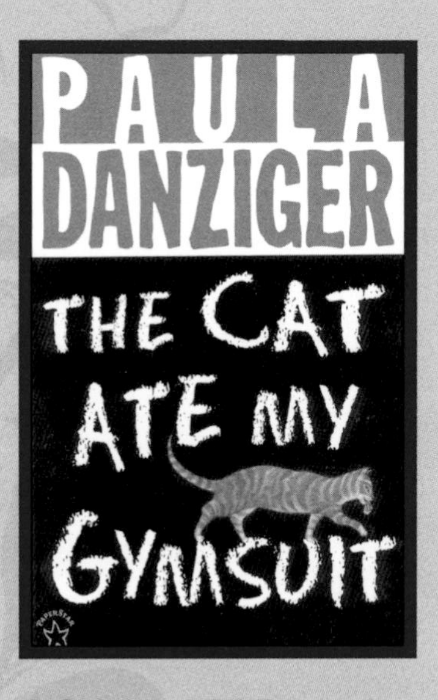

A Selected Bibliography of Danziger's Work

Get Ready for Second Grade, Amber Brown (2002)
It's Justin Time, Amber Brown (2001)
Snail Mail No More (with Ann M. Martin; 2000)
I, Amber Brown (1999)
Amber Brown Is Feeling Blue (1998)
P.S. Longer Letter Later (with Ann M. Martin; 1998)
Amber Brown Sees Red (1997)
Amber Brown Wants Extra Credit (1996)
Amber Brown Goes Fourth (1995)
Amber Brown Is Not a Crayon (1994)
Make Like a Tree and Leave (1990)
Everyone Else's Parents Said Yes (1989)
Remember Me to Harold Square (1987)
It's an Aardvark-Eat-Turtle World (1985)
The Divorce Express (1982)
There's a Bat in Bunk Five (1980)
Can You Sue Your Parents for Malpractice? (1979)
The Pistachio Prescription (1978)
The Cat Ate My Gymsuit (1974)

Amber Brown books as well as the teen novels *The Divorce Express, Can You Sue Your Parents for Malpractice?*, and *The Pistachio Prescription.* One reason for her popularity is her ability to think like her young characters. She starts by developing the characters instead of the storyline. She remembers things from her own childhood and draws on what she has learned from her students and other children in her life.

Danziger cares about the quality of her writing and works hard to do her best. She is friends with several other children's authors, including Ann M. Martin of the Baby-Sitters Club series, and often reads her work to them. Sometimes,

Danziger has young people read her manuscripts. "Most important to me is that writing allows me to use my sense of humor and sense of perspective. I hope that my books continue to help me grow and to help others grow," explains Danziger.

Paula Danziger loves to travel around the world and has visited schools in almost every state in the country. She lives in New York City.

Where to Find Out More About Paula Danziger

Books

Collier, Laurie, and Joyce Nakamura, eds. *Major Authors and Illustrators for Children and Young Adults.* Detroit: Gale Research, 1991.

Drew, Bernard A. *The 100 Most Popular Young Adult Authors: Biographical Sketches and Bibliographies.* Littleton, Colo.: Libraries Unlimited, 1996.

Krull, Katherine. *Presenting Paula Danziger.* New York: Twayne Publishers, 1995.

Web Sites

Educational Paperback Association
http://www.edupaperback.org/authorbios/Danziger_Paula.html
To read a biographical sketch and booklist for Paula Danziger

Scholastic Kids Fun Online
http://www.scholastic.com/titles/paula
To read about Paula Danziger's personality, travels, and career

Teenreads.com
http://www.teenreads.com/authors/au-danziger-paula.asp
To read a biographical sketch and an interview with Paula Danziger

---

Danziger doesn't follow a strict writing schedule. Some days she does no writing. Other days, she is at the computer mornings, afternoons, and evenings.

Bruce Degen

Born: June 14, 1945

Coming up with Ms. Frizzle's wild outfits is one of Bruce Degen's favorite things about illustrating the Magic School Bus series. He also loves drawing Ms. Frizzle's students, who are based on people he knew as a child.

Bruce Degen was born on June 14, 1945, in Brooklyn, New York. As a kid, he was always drawing. He also enjoyed reading science fiction and fantasy. At LaGuardia High School, Bruce concentrated on art. After that, he earned his bachelor of fine arts degree from Cooper Union in New York City. Then he got a master of fine arts degree from the Pratt Institute in Brooklyn.

Following his art education, Degen had jobs in many art-related fields. He painted scenery for operas, and he worked in advertising. He

---

Degen also writes some of the books he illustrates. He is the author of *Aunt Possum and the Pumpkin Man, The Little Witch and the Riddle, Jamberry, Teddy Bear Towers, Sailaway Home,* and *Daddy Is a Doodlebug.*

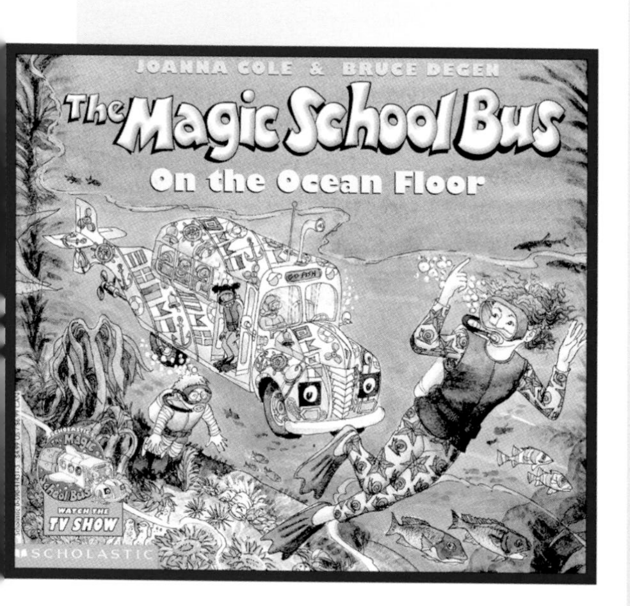

also made money by teaching art in high school and college.

Along the way, he realized he wasn't having fun. He thought about what he really liked about art—and decided to illustrate children's books. With this kind of work, Degen could enjoy himself, and his readers could share the fun.

Among the first books Bruce Degen illustrated were *Forecast and Caricatures* by

A Selected Bibliography of Degen's Work

Climb the Family Tree, Jesse Bear! (Illustrations only, 2002)
Ms. Frizzle's Adventures: Ancient Egypt (Illustrations only, 2001)
Daddy Is a Doodlebug (2000)
Liz Makes a Rainbow (Illustrations only, 1999)
What a Scare, Jesse Bear! (Illustrations only, 1999)
The Magic School Bus in the Arctic: A Book about Heat (Illustrations only, 1998)
Jesse Bear, What Will You Wear? (Illustrations only, 1996)
Sailaway Home (1996)
A Beautiful Feast for a Big King Cat (Illustrations only, 1994)
Will You Give Me a Dream? (Illustrations only, 1994)
Mouse's Birthday (Illustrations only, 1993)
The Magic School Bus on the Ocean Floor (1992)
Teddy Bear Towers (1991)
Dinosaur Dances (Illustrations only, 1990)
The Magic School Bus Lost in the Solar System (Illustrations only, 1990)
Lion and Lamb (Illustrations only, 1989)
If You Were a Writer (Illustrations only, 1988)
The Magic School Bus: Inside the Earth (Illustrations only, 1987)
The Josefina Story Quilt (Illustrations only, 1986)
The Magic School Bus at the Waterworks (Illustrations only, 1986)
Jamberry (1983)
Commander Toad and the Planet of the Grapes (Illustrations only, 1982)
Commander Toad in Space (Illustrations only, 1980)
The Little Witch and the Riddle (1980)
My Mother Didn't Kiss Me Goodnight (Illustrations only, 1980)
Caricatures (Illustrations only, 1978)
Aunt Possum and the Pumpkin Man (1977)
A Big Day for Scepters (Illustrations only, 1997)
Forecast (Illustrations only, 1977)

Degen's Major Literary Awards

1987 *Boston Globe–Horn Book* Nonfiction Honor Book
The Magic School Bus at the Waterworks

"The nice thing about books is that they go out into the world. When a kid, parent, or teacher tells you how much he or she likes your book, you realize that you've given something that has become part of someone else's life."

Malcolm Hall and *A Big Day for Scepters* by Stephen Krensky. Then he began using his watercolors and colored pencils to illustrate *Commander Toad in Space, Commander Toad and the Planet of the Grapes,* and other books in Jane Yolen's Commander Toad series. These books brought him recognition, but his real fame came later with the Magic School Bus series.

Starting with *The Magic School Bus at the Waterworks,* Degen and author Joanna Cole teamed up to make field trips more fun than ever. In this series, Ms. Frizzle and her students discover all sorts of amazing things about the ocean, weather, outer space, the human body, and all kinds of science. For the Magic School Bus books, Degen has worked with Cole and other authors to make learning more enjoyable for everyone.

"Since I began, this work has involved me totally, and I hope I will be doing it as long as I can hold a pencil."

In addition to working on the

Degen jokes that a fashion line based on Ms. Frizzle's outlandish clothing could be very popular.

Magic School Bus titles, Degen illustrates the Jesse Bear series written by Nancy White Carlstrom. He has also illustrated many other books for young readers. Bruce Degen lives in Connecticut with his family.

Where to Find Out More About Bruce Degen

Books

Kovacs, Deborah, and James Preller. *Meet the Authors and Illustrators: 60 Creators of Favorite Children's Books Talk about Their Work.* Vol. 1. New York: Scholastic, 1991.

Marcus, Leonard S. *Side by Side: Five Picture Book Teams Go to Work.* New York: Walker Books, 2001.

Web Sites

Magic School Bus Web Site from Scholastic
http://www.scholastic.com/magicschoolbus/home.htm
For games and an art gallery related to the popular television series

Scholastic Authors Online
http://www2.scholastic.com/teachers/authorsandbooks/authorstudies/authorhome.jhtml?authorID=26&collateralID=5139&displayName=Biography
To read an autobiographical sketch and selection of awards for Bruce Degen

Degen based the appearance of Ms. Frizzle on his high school geometry teacher.

Tomie de Paola

Born: September 15, 1934

When he was a little boy, Tomie de Paola promised himself that someday he would be an artist. He also wanted to be a writer. He kept his promises, writing and illustrating almost a hundred books for children, including the award-winning *Strega Nona: An Old Tale.*

Thomas Anthony de Paola was born on September 15, 1934, in Meriden, Connecticut, to Irish and Italian parents. His family encouraged his interest in art and his active imagination. His mother read many books to him and his brother. When he was ten years old, Tomie wrote

---

Several galleries and museums in the United States have exhibited de Paola's paintings and illustrations. His murals are on the walls of many Catholic churches and monasteries in New England.

books and gave them to his younger sisters as birthday presents.

> *"I showed my drawings to many people, especially those who were in charge of choosing artists to draw pictures for books for children. I showed them my drawings for six years! Finally, I was given a book to illustrate."*

Listening to a radio show also helped Tomie develop his imagination. "Growing up before television, I had what I can only consider the good fortune to be exposed to radio and I never missed that wonderful Saturday morning show, *Let's Pretend,*" de Paola explains.

Tomie knew he wanted to attend art school. After high school, he went to the Pratt Institute in Brooklyn, New York. He earned a bachelor of fine arts degree in 1956.

After college, de Paola entered a Benedictine Monastery in Vermont for six months. In the monastery, he had time to think and work on his art. He developed art for the monastery, designed fabric for the weaving studio, and designed Christmas cards.

In 1962, de Paola began teaching art at Newton College of the Sacred Heart in Massachusetts. Three years later, he illustrated his first book, *Sound,* written by Lisa Miller. In 1966, de Paola's *The Wonderful Dragon of Timlin* was published. It was the first book that de Paola both wrote and illustrated. The next year, he went to California to teach at

---

De Paola renovated a 200-year-old barn and uses it as his art studio. He has many of his books and illustrations on display there.

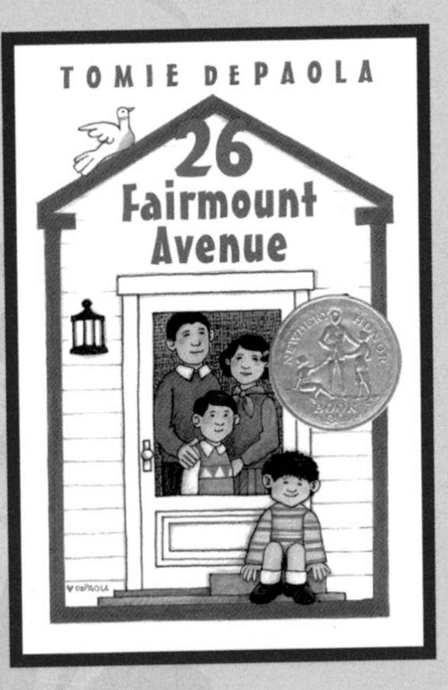

A Selected Bibliography of de Paola's Work

Adelita: A Mexican Cinderella Story (2002)
Boss for a Day (2001)
Here We All Are (2000)
Tomie de Paola's Rhyme Time (2000)
26 Fairmount Avenue (1999)
Days of the Blackbird: A Tale of Northern Italy (1997)
The Bubble Factory (1996)
Country Angel Christmas (1995)
Christopher: The Holy Giant (1994)
Kit and Kat (1994)
The Legend of the Persian Carpet (1993)
Jimmie O'Rourke and the Big Potato: An Irish Folktale (1992)
Little Grunt and the Big Egg: A Prehistoric Fairytale (1990)
The Art Lesson (1989)
Tomie de Paola's Mother Goose (1985)
Francis, the Poor Man of Assisi (1982)
The Friendly Beasts: An Old English Christmas Carol (1981)
The Quicksand Book (1977)
Strega Nona: An Old Tale (1975)
The Wonderful Dragon of Timlin (1966)
Sound (Illustrations only, 1965)

De Paola's Major Literary Awards

2000 Newbery Honor Book
26 Fairmount Avenue

1982 *Boston Globe–Horn Book* Picture Book Honor Book
The Friendly Beasts: An Old English Christmas Carol

1976 Caldecott Honor Book
Strega Nona: An Old Tale

Lone Mountain College near San Francisco. He earned a master's degree from the California College of Arts and Crafts before returning to Massachusetts.

While de Paola continued to teach art at various colleges, he also became involved in the theater. He designed costumes and sets for theater productions. He also taught college students how to design sets and write scripts for drama productions. De Paola worked on illustrations

"I never want to tell children things that aren't all true. I try to keep this promise in my stories, especially stories that are based on experiences in my own life."

for books by other authors and wrote and illustrated his own books.

Tomie de Paola has illustrated more than 110 books written by other authors. He has also written and illustrated more than 90 of his own children's books. Millions of copies of his books have been sold around the world. De Paola lives in New Hampshire and continues to write and illustrate children's books.

Where to Find Out More About Tomie de Paola

Books

Elleman, Barbara. *Tomie de Paola, His Art & His Stories.* New York: G. P. Putnam's Sons, 1999.

Kovacs, Deborah, and James Preller. *Meet the Authors and Illustrators: 60 Creators of Favorite Children's Books Talk about Their Work.* Vol. 1. New York: Scholastic, 1991.

Norby, Shirley. *Famous Children's Authors.* Minneapolis: T. S. Denison & Company, 1988.

Web Sites

Educational Paperback Association
http://www.edupaperback.org/authorbios/De Paola_Tomie.html
To read an autobiographical sketch and booklist for Tomie de Paola

Tomie de Paola's Web Site
http://www.bingley.com/
For biographical information about Tomie de Paola and de Paola's tour schedule

---

Many of de Paola's stories have been made into video and sound recordings. Children's theater companies have produced and performed many of his plays.

David Diaz

Born: 1958

Illustrator David Diaz uses many techniques to bring stories to life. He works in acrylic, watercolor, ink, and other mediums, and he is always willing to try new ideas. His creativity helps makes his books inviting and memorable.

David Diaz was born in Fort Lauderdale, Florida, in 1958. Growing up, he was always artistic. In high school, David met his future wife, Cecelia, in an art class. Together they learned about color and its uses.

One of David's art instructors in high school gave him lots of encouragement. She urged him to enter his artwork in competitions, and

David Diaz's first job in California was working at a drive-up window where people dropped off film to be developed.

she explained all the different work that artists can do.

After high school, Diaz attended the Fort Lauderdale Art Institute. Then he and Cecelia moved to San Diego, California.

Diaz's first job as an illustrator was for a weekly newspaper called the *San Diego Reader*. Then he did illustrations for corporations and national publications. His artwork has also appeared in advertisements for products such as Pepsi and Perrier.

> *"When I was in the first grade, I knew I wanted to be an artist—although I had no idea what an illustrator, designer, or art director was."*

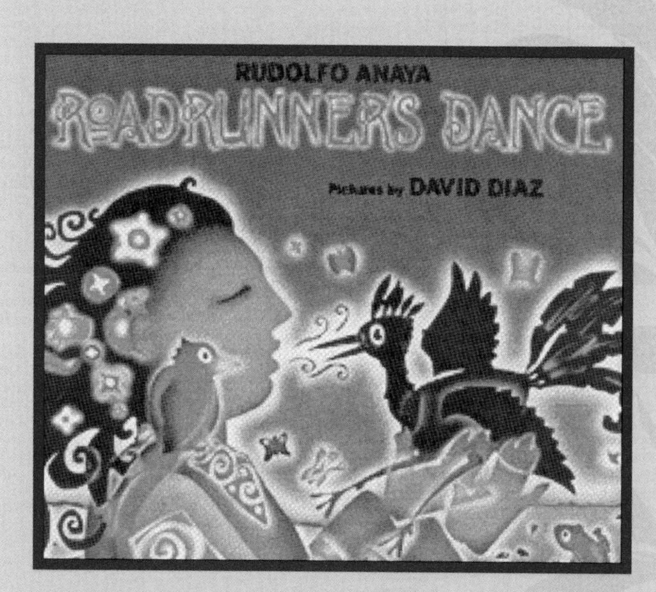

A Selected Bibliography of Diaz's Work

The Pot That Juan Built (2002)
Angel Face (2001)
The Gospel Cinderella (2000)
Jump Rope Magic (2000)
Roadrunner's Dance (2000)
The Wanderer (2000)
Shadow Story (1999)
Be Not Far from Me: The Oldest Love Story: Legends from the Bible (1998)
The Disappearing Alphabet (1998)
The Little Scarecrow Boy (1998)
The Christmas Home (1997)
December (1997)
Going Home (1996)
The Inner City Mother Goose (1996)
Just One Flick of a Finger (1996)
Wilma Unlimited: How Wilma Rudolph Became the World's Fastest Woman (1996)
Smoky Night (1994)
Neighborhood Odes (1992)

Diaz's Major Literary Awards

1995 Caldecott Medal
Smoky Night

The first children's book that Diaz illustrated was *Neighborhood Odes,* a collection of poems by Gary Soto. Then came *Smoky Night,* a picture book by Eve Bunting about the Los Angeles riots. For *Smoky Night,* Diaz used an interesting collage style with varying textures and rich colors. In 1995, Diaz won the Caldecott Medal for *Smoky Night.* This is one of highest honors a children's book illustrator can receive.

"I don't want to lose my audience [by using different styles], but I think that by changing techniques I add more interest to the books that I do."

Since then, Diaz has illustrated more books by Bunting and a host of other authors. Among his varied titles are *The Inner City Mother Goose* by Eve Merriam; *Wilma Unlimited: How Wilma Rudolph Became the World's Fastest Woman* by Kathleen Krull; and *Be Not Far from Me: The Oldest Love Story: Legends from the Bible* retold by Eric A. Kimmel. Diaz enjoys working on a variety of books and likes to experiment with new techniques and styles.

Cecelia Diaz says that while her husband is artistic in all that he does, he is most driven by his love for his family. David and Cecelia Diaz live in Rancho La Costa, California, with their daughter and two sons.

BEFORE DIAZ AGREES TO ILLUSTRATE A BOOK, HIS WIFE, CECILIA, READS THE MANUSCRIPT. IF SHE LIKES IT, HE READS IT AND CONSIDERS THE PROJECT. IF SHE DOESN'T, HE TURNS THE PROJECT DOWN.

Where to Find Out More About David Diaz

Books

Holtze, Sally Holmes, ed. *Seventh Book of Junior Authors & Illustrators.* New York: H. W. Wilson Company, 1996.

Something about the Author. Vol. 96. Detroit: Gale Research, 1998.

Web Sites

HOUGHTON MIFFLIN: MEET THE ILLUSTRATOR
http://www.eduplace.com/kids/hmr/mtai/diaz.html
To read a biographical sketch and booklist for David Diaz

SCHOLASTIC AUTHORS ONLINE
http://www2.scholastic.com/teachers/authorsandbooks/authorstudies/authorhome.jhtml?authorID=28&collateralID=5145&displayName=Biography
For an autobiographical sketch by David Diaz, a booklist, and the transcript of an interview

---

Before he began illustrating children's books, Diaz created a book called *Sweet Peas,* a collection of illustrations of the faces of people he observed during a trip down the Amazon River.

Kate DiCamillo

Born: March 25, 1964

Imagine being homesick during the long winter months in Minnesota. What would you do? Well, if you were author Kate DiCamillo, you would write a story about a girl growing up in the warm sunshine of Florida.

Kate DiCamillo was born on March 25, 1964, in Merion, Pennsylvania. During her sickly childhood, Kate read lots of books. Her favorites were *A Secret Garden, The Yearling,* and all of Beverly Cleary's Ramona books. In time, Kate's family moved south to the small town of Clermont, Florida, to help her recover from chronic pneumonia.

When she became an adult, DiCamillo moved to Minneapolis, Minnesota. She wrote her first novel, *Because of Winn-Dixie,* during one

WHEN DICAMILLO WAS WRITING ***BECAUSE OF WINN-DIXIE,*** SHE WAS LIVING IN AN APARTMENT BUILDING THAT DID NOT ALLOW DOGS. IT WAS THE FIRST TIME SHE HAD EVER LIVED WITHOUT A DOG.

of those cold winters in Minnesota. Winn-Dixie was the grocery store where Kate shopped when she lived in Clermont. It is also where her main character, India Opal Buloni, finds a stray dog. She names the dog Winn-Dixie, and they become best friends. "The book is (I hope) a hymn of praise to dogs, friendship, and the South," explains DiCamillo.

"Writing is seeing the world. It is paying attention."

Other parts of DiCamillo's childhood also find their way into her stories. She grew up with her mother and brother but not her father. He left the family when she was young. Several of DiCamillo's main characters have lived in single-parent families. She says she knows how it feels to live without both parents at home.

In 1987, DiCamillo earned a bachelor's degree in English from the University of Florida in Gainesville. Her college classes helped her learn about reading. But she did not become a writer until she was twenty-eight. That was when she decided she had to start writing every day. Now DiCamillo sets a goal of writing two pages every morning, after a cup of coffee. Most mornings, she goes to work at a bookstore after she writes.

Working at the bookstore helped DiCamillo decide to write for

---

DICAMILLO FIRST CREATED ROB, THE MAIN CHARACTER IN *THE TIGER RISING,* AS A CHARACTER IN A SHORT STORY. THEN SHE DECIDED HE STILL HAD MORE OF A STORY TO TELL, SO HE BECAME THE MAIN CHARACTER IN HER BOOK.

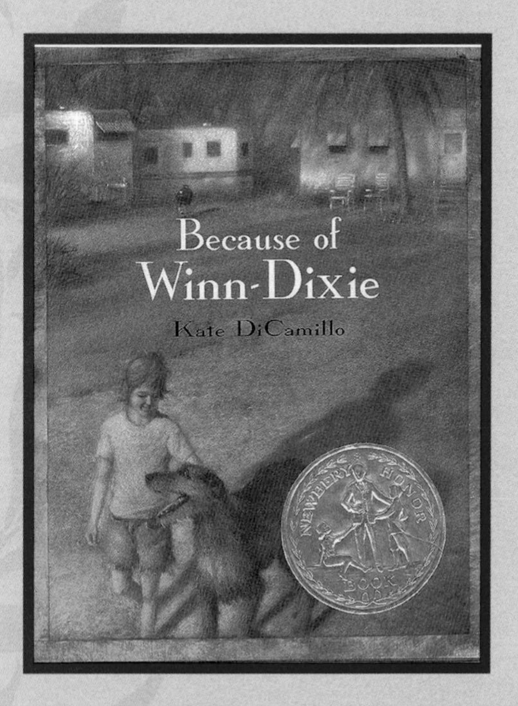

A Selected Bibliography of DiCamillo's Work

The Tiger Rising (2001)
Because of Winn-Dixie (2000)

DiCamillo's Major Literary Awards

2001 Newbery Honor Book
Because of Winn-Dixie

children. She began to read some of the children's books at the store. She was so impressed by some of the stories that she wanted to try it herself. Some of DiCamillo's work has been published in magazines for children. She also writes short stories for adults, but writing for children is her favorite. In 2001, DiCamillo published her second book, *The Tiger Rising,* about a twelve-year-old boy who finds a tiger in the woods.

Some people think that writing for children is easy. DiCamillo knows it is not. She spends lots of time rewriting and revising her stories. She rewrote *Because of Winn-Dixie* eight times! DiCamillo also knows that paying attention to detail is important. So she rewrites her stories until she has every detail right.

> *"It's wonderful to tell stories and have people listen to them."*

Kate DiCamillo believes that one of the best things about having her books published is that she now gets letters from children. She says her biggest thrill is to have a child ask her to write another book. She tells children that reading books can change their lives.

Where to Find Out More about Kate DiCamillo

Books

Something about the Author. Vol. 121. Detroit: Gale Research, 2001.

Web Sites

BookBrowse.com
http://www.bookbrowse.com/dyn_/author/authorID/573.htm
To read an article about Kate DiCamillo

KidsReads.com
http://www.kidsreads.com/authors/au-dicamillo-kate.asp
To read an interview with Kate DiCamillo

DiCamillo got the idea to write *The Tiger Rising* after her mother showed her a newspaper article about a tiger that had escaped from the circus.

Leo Dillon
Diane Dillon

Born: March 2, 1933 (Leo)
Born: March 13, 1933 (Diane)

Leo and Diane Dillon have been illustrating books together for more than forty years. They have illustrated more than fifty children's books for other authors including *Why Mosquitoes Buzz in People's Ears; Ashanti to Zulu: African Traditions;* and *Aïda.* The Dillons have also created illustrations for posters, advertisements, and album covers.

Leo and Diane were both born in 1933—in different parts of the country. Diane was born on March 13 in Glendale, California. Leo was born on March 2 in Brooklyn, New York.

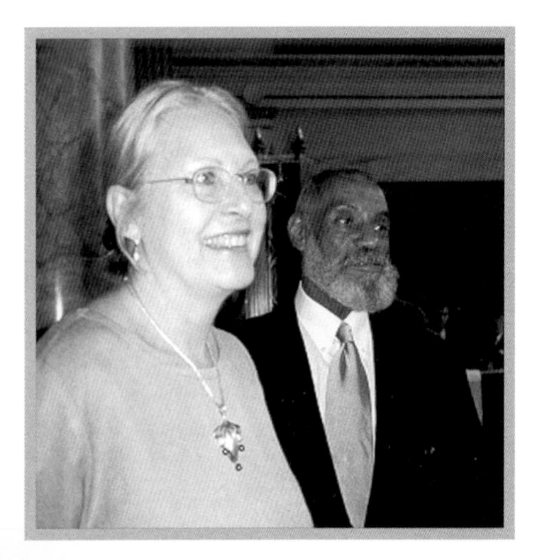

Leo and Diane met in 1953 as students at the Parsons School of Design in New York City. They had seen each other's art

Diane Dillon created a stained glass ceiling that was installed in the Eagle Gallery in New York City.

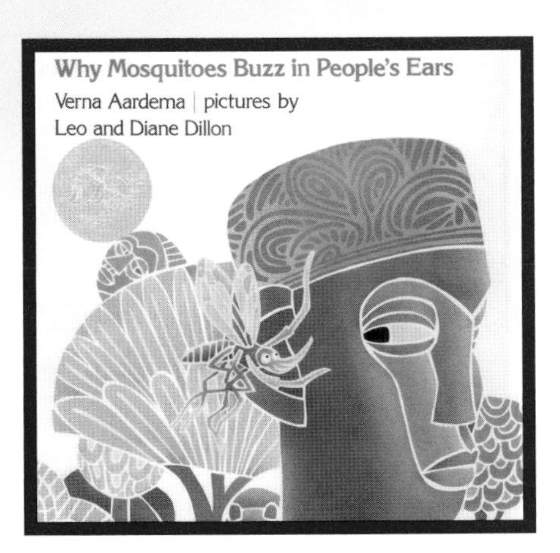

before they actually met. After they met, they competed to see who was the better artist.

The Dillons began working together shortly after they married in 1957. They established their own company called Studio 2. The first children's book they illustrated was *Hakon of Rogen's Saga.* The book, written by Erik C. Haugaard, was published in 1963.

The Dillons have illustrated books by many other children's authors. Their work

A Selected Bibliography of the Dillons' Work

Rap a Tap Tap (2002)

Mansa Musa: The Lion of Mali (2001)

Two Little Trains (2001)

The Girl Who Spun Gold (2000)

Wind Child (1999)

Her Stories: African American Folktales, Fairy Tales, and True Tales (1995)

Switch on the Night (1993)

Northern Lullaby (1992)

Aïda (1991)

The Tale of the Mandarin Ducks (1989)

The People Could Fly: American Black Folktales (1985)

Who's in Rabbit's House?: A Masai Tale (1977)

Ashanti to Zulu: African Traditions (1976)

The Hundred Penny Box (1975)

Song of the Boat (1975)

Why Mosquitoes Buzz in People's Ears (1975)

The Ring in the Prairie: A Shawnee Legend (1970)

Hakon of Rogen's Saga (1963)

The Dillons' Major Literary Awards

1996 Coretta Scott King Illustrator Honor Book
Her Stories: African American Folktales, Fairy Tales, and True Tales

1991 *Boston Globe–Horn Book* Picture Book Award
The Tale of the Mandarin Ducks

1991 Coretta Scott King Illustrator Award
Aïda

1986 Coretta Scott King Illustrator Honor Book
The People Could Fly: American Black Folktales

1977 *Boston Globe–Horn Book* Picture Book Honor Book
1977 Caldecott Medal
Ashanti to Zulu: African Traditions

1976 *Boston Globe–Horn Book* Picture Book Honor Book
Song of the Boat

1976 Caldecott Medal
Why Mosquitoes Buzz in People's Ears

1975 *Boston Globe–Horn Book* Fiction Honor Book
The Hundred Penny Box

"Together we are ableto create art that we would not be able to do individually."
—Leo and Diane Dillon

has won them many awards, including the Caldecott Medal and the Coretta Scott King Illustrator Award. The Dillons were the first illustrators to win the Caldecott Medal two years in a row—in 1976 and in 1977.

Leo and Diane Dillon have a collaborative approach to their work. Leo might work on a sketch and then pass it to Diane. Then she might add something and pass it back to Leo. When the illustration is complete, it is a combination of their ideas. The Dillons refer to this process as "the third artist" because the final work is something they probably couldn't have created on their own. "At the point we hit the 'third artist' concept, it helped us a lot, because we could look at ourselves as an artist rather than two individuals," Diane Dillon explains.

"Art in its many forms has survived to inform us of lives long gone. Art inspires, lifts our spirits, and brings beauty to our lives. We wish to pay homage to it and the people that created it."
—Leo and Diane Dillon

The Dillons' illustrations

Leo Dillon was the first African-American to win the Caldecott Medal. He won the medal with Diane in 1976 for their illustrations in *Why Mosquitoes Buzz in People's Ears.*

are often a combination of art techniques. They sometimes have to learn new techniques for a book. Other times, they invent their own. "We take great pride in illustration and the fact that we are illustrators," Diane Dillon says. "We've never thought there is a difference between 'fine art' and illustration other than good art or bad art."

The Dillons continue to create illustrations for children's books. They have a son and live in New York City.

Where to Find Out More about Leo and Diane Dillon

Books

Kovacs, Deborah, and James Preller. *Meet the Authors and Illustrators: 60 Creators Children's Books Talk about Their Work.* Vol. 1. New York: Scholastic, 1991.

Sutherland, Zena. *Children & Books.* 9th ed. New York: Addison Wesley Longman, 1997.

Web Sites

Scholastic Authors Online
http://www2.scholastic.com/teachers/authorsandbooks/authorstudies/authorhome.jhtml?authorID=210&collateralID=5146&displayName=Biography
To read a biographical sketch of Leo and Diane Dillon

The Dillons' son, Lionel John Dillon III, is a painter, sculptor, and jewelry craftsperson. He has also worked with his parents on the illustrations for several books.

Michael Dorris

Born: January 30, 1945
Died: April 11, 1997

Michael Dorris was part Modoc Indian. He did many kinds of work—teaching, research, and writing nonfiction and fiction for adults and children. His concern for Native Americans was part of almost everything he did during his life.

Michael Dorris was born on January 30, 1945, in Louisville, Kentucky. His father was killed in World War II (1938–1945), and Michael lived with his mother, grandmother, and aunt, except for a little time he spent on a reservation in Montana.

After high school, Dorris went to Georgetown University in Washington, D.C. Then he got a graduate degree in anthropology at Yale University in New Haven, Connecticut. Part of Dorris's research involved

---

MICHAEL DORRIS GOT THE IDEA FOR HIS FIRST YOUNG ADULT NOVEL, *MORNING GIRL,* WHEN HE STARTED WONDERING ABOUT A YOUNG TAINO GIRL MENTIONED IN AN ENTRY IN CHRISTOPHER COLUMBUS'S DIARY.

living in a fishing village in Alaska.

In Alaska, Dorris adopted a three-year-old Sioux boy named Abel. He became one of the first unmarried men in the United States to adopt a child. Eventually Dorris adopted two other Indian children.

> *"When I was growing up . . . I rarely encountered Native American fictional characters with whom I could identify. The native peoples I read about in books always seemed to be performing rather dull crafts—sort of like earnest Boy Scouts—or riding around on ponies bareback, whooping it up."*

In 1979, Dorris started a department dedicated to Native American studies at Dartmouth University in Hanover, New Hampshire. At Dartmouth, he met Louise Erdrich, a student who was also part Indian and interested in writing. The two married in 1981. Michael Dorris and Louise Erdrich became one of the best-known literary couples in the United States.

Erdrich's fiction, starting with *Love Medicine* in 1985, concerned Native Americans. Dorris also published a novel, but it was his nonfiction book *The Broken Cord* that became a bestseller. In *The Broken Cord,* Dorris wrote about the struggle to help his adopted son, Abel, who suffered from fetal alcohol syndrome (FAS). FAS is a combination of birth defects that tend to occur in babies whose mothers drink large amounts of alcohol during pregnancy. *The Broken Cord* informed people

DORRIS OPPOSED USING INDIAN NAMES FOR PRODUCTS AND SPORTS TEAMS. WHEN HE WAS AT DARTMOUTH UNIVERSITY, HE SPENT FIFTEEN YEARS TRYING TO GET THE DARTMOUTH INDIANS TO CHANGE THEIR NAME. TODAY, THE TEAM IS KNOWN AS THE BIG GREEN.

A Selected Bibliography of Dorris's Work

The Window (1997)
Sees Behind Trees (1996)
Guests (1994)
Morning Girl (1992)

Dorris's Major Literary Awards

1993 Scott O'Dell Award
Morning Girl

about the plight of children with FAS and the dangers of drinking during pregnancy.

Dorris kept writing novels and short stories for adults. He also began to write for young people. Dorris's first children's book, *Morning Girl,* was published in 1992—500 years after Christopher Columbus discovered America. This book of historical fiction tells about the lives of a young brother and sister who are Taino Indians—the first people that Columbus met in the Americas.

More novels followed. *Guests* is about an Indian boy who is unhappy that his father has invited European colonists to their harvest feast. In *Sees Behind Trees,* a Native American boy wants to become a hunter but has to learn to overcome his nearsightedness.

In spite of his success, Michael Dorris suffered from depression. On April 11, 1997, he took his own life in Concord, New Hampshire. His young adult book *The Window* was published after his death in 1997.

"There are many things that Indian people are not:. . . .They are not represented by the stereotypes of Hollywood or most fiction; they are not people without history, languages, literatures, sciences, and arts; they are not vanished, and are not vanishing."

Where to Find Out More About Michael Dorris

Books

Holtze, Sally Holmes, ed. *Seventh Book of Junior Authors & Illustrators.* New York: H. W. Wilson Company, 1996.

Weil, Ann. *Michael Dorris.* Austin, Texas: Raintree/Steck-Vaughn, 1997.

Web Sites

E Museum: Michael Dorris
http://emuseum.mnsu.edu/information/biography/abcde/dorris_michael.html
To read a brief biographical sketch of Michael Dorris

Scholastic Authors Online
http://www2.scholastic.com/teachers/authorsandbooks/authorstudies/authorhome.jhtml?authorID=30&collateralID=5150&displayName=Biography
For an autobiographical sketch by Michael Dorris, a booklist, and a transcript an interview

---

Dorris's favorite author as a child was his mother. She "made up new stories every night. None of them were written down but all of them were magical and special because they were just for me," Dorris said.

Arthur Dorros

Born: May 19, 1950

Many authors write about experiences they have had themselves. Author and illustrator Arthur Dorros does exactly that in his books. For example, Dorros lived in South America for a year and used his experience to write *Tonight Is Carnaval,* a story about a South American family getting ready to celebrate Carnaval.

Arthur Dorros speaks English and Spanish and writes in both languages. He wants children in the United States to know about life in other countries. One of Dorros's books, *This Is My House,* shows the different types of houses that children live in all over the world. On each page the words "This is my house" are written in the language spoken in the country featured.

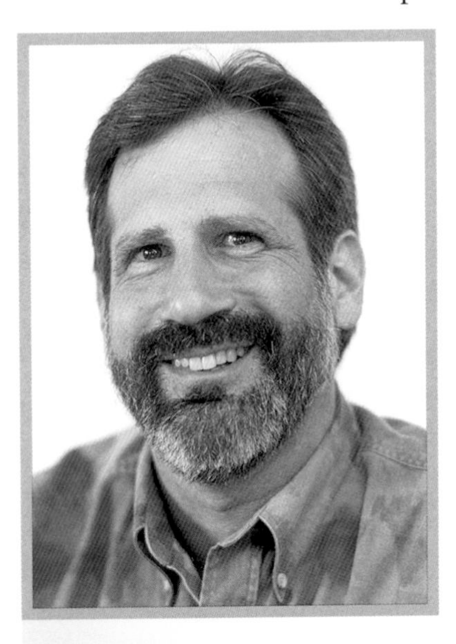

Another of Arthur Dorros's books mixes Spanish phrases with an English text. *Abuela,*

When he was four years old, Arthur Dorros sat on the tail of a ten-foot alligator. He used this experience to write his second book, *Alligator Shoes.*

which means "grandmother" in Spanish, is the story of a girl named Rosalba who dreams that she and her grandmother fly together over New York City. A second book, *Isla,* continues the story of Rosalba and Abuela. The grandmother and granddaughter visit the Caribbean island where Abuela grew up. Dorros drew on his close relationship with his own grandmother to write these stories.

Because he loves nature, Dorros also writes and illustrates nonfiction science books for

> *"I believe you can achieve what you want, if you're willing to work at it, and have fun at the same time."*

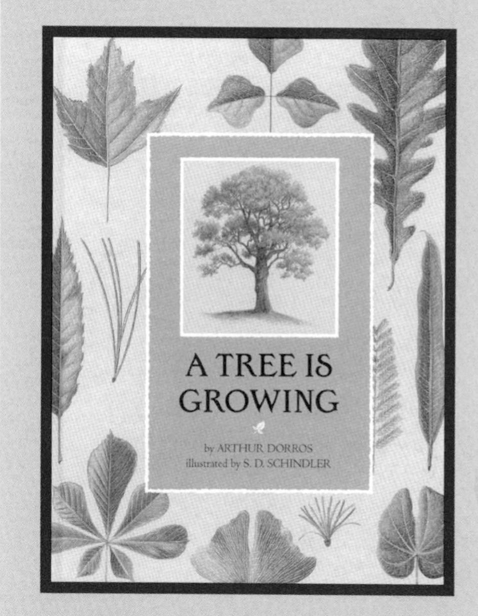

A Selected Bibliography of Dorros's Work

City Chicken (2002)
When the Pigs Took Over (2002)
The Fungus That Ate My School (2000)
Ten Go Tango (2000)
A Tree Is Growing (1997)
Isla (1995)
Elephant Families (1994)
Radio Man=Don Radio: A Story in English and Spanish (1993)
This Is My House (1992)
Abuela (1991)
Animal Tracks (1991)
Follow the Water from Brook to Ocean (1991)
Tonight Is Carnaval (1991)
Magic Secrets (Illustrations only, 1990)
Me and My Shadow (1990)
Rain Forest Secrets (1990)
Feel the Wind (1989)
Ant Cities (1987)
What Makes Day and Night (Illustrations only, 1986)
Charlie's House (Illustrations only, 1983)
Alligator Shoes (1982)
Pretzels (1981)

Dorros's Major Literary Awards

1998 Orbis Pictus Honor Book
A Tree Is Growing

young children. He has written books about ants, elephants, water, and the wind. The National Science Teachers Association selected three of his books—*Ant Cities, Feel the Wind,* and *Rain Forest Secrets*—as outstanding science books. Another book, *A Tree Is Growing,* won an award from the American Horticultural Society in 1998.

"I wasn't born an author. I had to learn . . . [that you] have to keep on trying and don't let anyone make you stop."

Born on May 19, 1950, Arthur Dorros grew up in Washington, D.C. He loved to read and draw when he was young. He says his father was a great storyteller. Arthur's mother kept bottles of tempera paint and other art supplies on hand for him.

In high school, Arthur became hooked on drawing when he had to draw amoebas and other creatures as part of his biology assignments. Later, he became hooked on telling stories to children in his neighborhood. He finally put the two things he enjoyed the most—storytelling and drawing—together. He created his first picture book, *Pretzels,* when he was twenty-nine.

Before he became a published writer, Arthur Dorros had many other jobs. He was a carpenter, an elementary school teacher, a farm-

ARTHUR DORROS LOVED DRAWING WHEN HE WAS A CHILD, BUT GAVE IT UP IN FIFTH GRADE BECAUSE HE THOUGHT HE WAS NOT VERY GOOD! NOW HE TELLS CHILDREN TO KEEP TRYING THINGS EVEN IF THEY MAKE A MISTAKE.

worker, and a photographer. He enjoys meeting people and learning about them. These different jobs helped him prepare for his career as a writer. He thinks that a good writer or illustrator is like a detective. A detective looks for clues to solve a mystery; a writer looks for clues to tell a good story.

Where to Find Out More About Arthur Dorros

Books

Holtze, Sally Holmes, ed. *Seventh Book of Junior Authors & Illustrators.* New York: H. W. Wilson Company, 1996.

Something about the Author. Vol. 122. Detroit: Gale Research, 2001.

Web Sites

Arthur Dorros's Web Site
http://www.arthurdorros.com/
To read an autobiographical account by Arthur Dorros and information about his books

Penguin Putnam Authors
http://www.penguinputnam.com/Author/AuthorFrame?0000006902
For information about Arthur Dorros's life

Dorros has lived in many places in the United States, from one coast to the other. He was born in Washington, D.C., and graduated from the University of Wisconsin. Now he lives on the West Coast, in Seattle, Washington.

Lois Duncan

Born: April 28, 1934

Even as a young child, Lois Duncan knew she wanted to be a writer. When she was just ten years old, Lois began sending stories to magazines. At the age of thirteen, she sold her first story for twenty-five dollars! In 1958, she wrote her first full-length novel, *Debutante Hill.* Since then, Lois has penned more than forty books.

Some of Duncan's best-loved novels are eerie mysteries for young adults. Several of Duncan's chilling stories have inspired made-for-TV movies and feature films. *Summer of Fear, Killing Mr. Griffin,* and *Don't Look Behind You* were made into television movies. *I Know What You Did Last Summer* was released as a feature film in 1997.

Lois Duncan was born in Philadelphia, Pennsylvania, on April 28, 1934. Her parents, Joseph and Lois Steinmetz, were magazine photographers. They both encouraged Lois's love of storytelling. When

Lois Duncan hated the movie version of *I Know What You Did Last Summer.* She felt that it was much too violent.

Lois was just a toddler, her parents wrote down and saved the stories she made up for them. Lois and her parents moved to Sarasota, Florida, when her brother, Billy, was born.

> ***"Writing gives you the power to create whole worlds and make everything in them happen the way you want it to."***

Growing up, Lois was a shy bookworm who wore braces and eyeglasses. To help her through her teen years, Lois poured her thoughts and feelings into stories. When she wasn't given a part in the school play, for example, she wrote a story in which she won the starring role.

As an adult, Duncan found that she could earn a living by writing. After her first marriage ended in 1961, she moved with her three small children to Albuquerque, New Mexico, to be near her brother. Duncan supported her family by writing magazine articles. Once she remarried, however, she turned her attention to the kind of writing she loved best: fiction for young adults.

In 1966, Duncan wrote *Ransom,* her first young adult suspense novel. *Ransom* was a hit with teens who loved spine-tingling mysteries. It was also a runner-up for the Edgar Allan Poe Award, a prize given for outstanding mystery writing. Since then, each novel Duncan writes earns her new fans. Teens love her stories' supernatural twists and realistic teenage characters.

OVER THE YEARS, LOIS DUNCAN HAS RECEIVED MANY AWARDS FOR HER WRITING. IN 1992, SHE WON THE MARGARET E. EDWARDS AWARD FOR OUTSTANDING TEEN FICTION.

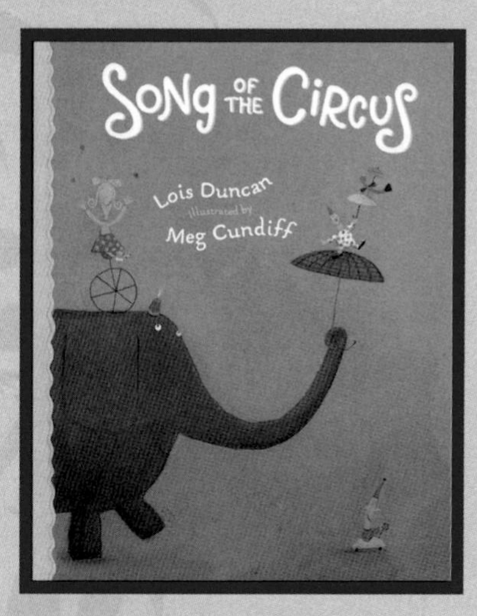

A Selected Bibliography of Duncan's Work

Song of the Circus (2002)
I Walk at Night (2000)
The Longest Hair in the World (1999)
Gallows Hill (1997)
The Magic of Spider Woman (1996)
Who Killed My Daughter? (1992)
The Birthday Moon (1989)
Don't Look Behind You (1989)
They Never Came Home (1989)
The Twisted Window (1987)
Locked in Time (1985)
The Third Eye (1984)
The Terrible Tales of Happy Days School (1983)
Chapters: My Growth As a Writer (1982)
Stranger with My Face (1981)
Daughters of Eve (1979)
Killing Mr. Griffin (1978)
Summer of Fear (1976)
Down a Dark Hall (1974)
I Know What You Did Last Summer (1973)
A Gift of Magic (1971)
Hotel for Dogs (1971)
Peggy (1970)
Ransom (1966)
Season of the Two-Heart (1964)
Game of Danger (1962)
Debutante Hill (1958)

Lois Duncan has never forgotten the advice of a friend who told her to write about what she knows. Many of her books are set in the Southwest or near the ocean—places where Duncan has lived. Over the years, Duncan has tried different styles of writing. She has written nonfiction books for both adults and young adults. She wrote picture books for her grandchildren to enjoy. She has also written books of poetry. In 1982, Duncan even published her autobiography.

"Sometimes I feel that I am two people in one, with a part of me living each experience and another part observing."

In 1989, personal tragedy struck: Duncan's eighteen-year-old daughter, Kaitlyn, was shot to death while driving. Officials determined that the killing was a random shooting, but Duncan was unconvinced. In 1992, Duncan wrote the book *Who Killed My Daughter?* She hopes that the book might encourage someone to provide information to help find her daughter's killer. "It's not a matter of revenge. It's a matter of Kait being worth the truth," she explains.

Since the loss of her daughter, Duncan has written several books. She continues to tell fascinating stories for people of all ages. Fans of Duncan's work can count on more books in the future. For this award-winning author, writing is like breathing.

Where to Find Out More About Lois Duncan

Books

Duncan, Lois. *Chapters: My Growth As a Writer.* Boston: Little, Brown, 1982.

Kies, Cosette. *Presenting Lois Duncan.* New York: Twayne Publishers, 1993.

Web Sites

Lois Duncan's Web Site
http://loisduncan.arquettes.com
To read a booklist and a letter from Lois Duncan to her fans

Random House Authors/Illustrators
http://www.randomhouse.com/teachers/authors/dunc.html
To read a biographical account of Lois Duncan

Lois Duncan often creates characters based on people she knows. In fact, some of characters in past books were based on her children.

Richard Egielski

Born: July 16, 1952

*trange.* That is the word that author and illustrator Richard Egielski heard when he first tried to sell his drawings. Some editors thought his drawings were too strange for children's books. Few people think that now. Egielski has illustrated more than thirty children's books and has won many awards.

Richard Egielski was born on July 16, 1952, in New York City. His father was a police lieutenant and his mother was a secretary. His parents called him the artist of the family. Richard began to really study art when he was a

RICHARD EGIELSKI STARTS HIS DRAWINGS WITH A PENCIL. LATER HE GOES BACK OVER THEM WITH WATERCOLOR. HE TRIES TO COMPLETE TWO BOOKS A YEAR.

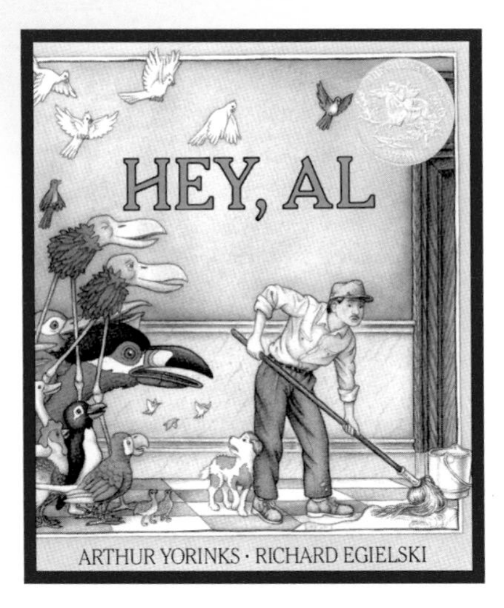

teenager at the High School of Art and Design, a public school in New York City.

Later Egielski studied at the Parsons School of Design. He thought he might become a commercial artist. Then he took a class in picture books taught by Maurice Sendak, the famous children's book author. Sendak inspired Egielski to become an illustrator for children's books.

At the Parsons School of Design, Richard Egielski met

A Selected Bibliography of Egielski's Work

Locust Pocus: A Book to Bug You (Illustrations only, 2001)
Three Magic Balls (2000)
The Web Files (Illustrations only, 2000)
One Present from Flekman's (Illustrations only, 1999)
The Tub People's Christmas (Illustrations only, 1999)
Jazper (1998)
The Gingerbread Boy (1997)
Perfect Pancakes, If You Please (Illustrations only, 1997)
Fire! Fire! Said Mrs. McGuire (Illustrations only, 1996)
Buz (1995)
Call Me Ahnighito (Illustrations only, 1995)
The Tub Grandfather (Illustrations only, 1993)
The Lost Sailor (Illustrations only, 1992)
Christmas in July (Illustrations only, 1991)
A Telling of the Tales: Five Stories (Illustrations only, 1990)
Oh, Brother (Illustrations only, 1989)
The Tub People (Illustrations only, 1989)
Bravo, Minski (Illustrations only, 1988)
Friends Forever (Illustrations only, 1988)
Hey, Al (Illustrations only, 1986)
Amy's Eyes (Illustrations only, 1985)
Lower! Higher! You're a Liar! (Illustrations only, 1984)
Getting Even (Illustrations only, 1982)
Mary's Mirror (Illustrations only, 1982)
Mr. Wheatfield's Loft (Illustrations only, 1981)
Finders Weepers (Illustrations only, 1980)
Louis the Fish (Illustrations only, 1980)
I Should Worry, I Should Care (Illustrations only, 1979)
Sid & Sol (Illustrations only, 1977)
The Letter, the Witch, and the Ring (Illustrations only, 1976)
The Porcelain Pagoda (Illustrations only, 1976)

Egielski's Major Literary Awards

1987 Caldecott Medal
Hey, Al

"An important teacher is one who exposes you to something new and points out a direction you otherwise might have missed."

another illustrator—Denise Saldutti. They married in 1977, three years after Egielski graduated.

Like many authors, Egielski uses experiences from his own life in his books. One time he had Lyme disease. The doctor gave him some medicine to get rid of the bug that was making him sick. Egielski liked the idea of a bug so he used it in the first book that he wrote and illustrated, *Buz.* This story is about a boy who swallows a bug when he is eating his breakfast. The doctor gives the boy some pills to track down the bug in the boy's body. Another of his books, *Jazper,* tells the story of a young boy insect and his father who live in a rented eggshell. The *New York Times* named *Jazper* the best illustrated book of 1998.

"A good illustrator is never a slave to text. The text rarely tells him what to do, but, rather, what his choices are. I only illustrate texts I truly believe in."

Sometimes Richard Egielski works with a partner to make a book. For *Sid & Sol,* Egielski did the illustrations and Arthur Yorinks wrote the text. One of Egielski's former art teachers had told Yorinks about Egielski's drawings and suggested they work together on a project. So they did. Over a period of four-

RICHARD EGIELSKI ENJOYS PLAYING THE MANDOLIN, A STRINGED INSTRUMENT.

teen years, the two men worked on eight books together. One of their books, *Hey, Al,* won the Caldecott Medal in 1987.

Richard Egielski also illustrated a series of books by author Pam Conrad. Conrad wrote stories about the Tub People, a family that lives in a bathroom. Egielski's and Conrad's first book together, *The Tub People,* won the Parents' Choice Picture Book Award in 1989.

"It is through my illustrations that I express myself most deeply and fully," Egielski explains. The illustrator lives in New York City, where he happily continues to create his "strange" drawings.

Where to Find Out More About Richard Egielski

Books

Cummings, Pat, ed. *Talking with Artists.* 1st ed. New York: Macmillan, 1992.

Holtze, Sally Holmes, ed. *Sixth Book of Junior Authors & Illustrators.* New York: H. W. Wilson Company, 1989.

Silvey, Anita, ed. *Children's Books and Their Creators.* Boston: Houghton Mifflin, 1995.

Web Sites

BookPeople
http://www.bookpeople.com/infobook.html?isbn=egielskipg
To see samples of Egielski's artwork and descriptions of his books

---

In 1997, Richard Egielski wrote and illustrated *The Gingerbread Boy,* based on the classic nursery rhyme. In this version, the gingerbread boy is in New York, and rats, police on horseback, and construction workers chase him!

Lois Ehlert

Born: November 9, 1934

Lois Ehlert creates beautiful picture books for children. Many of them she has written herself. Some of them she has illustrated for other writers. Children and adults have been enjoying her books for thirty years. Ehlert's best-known books include *Color Zoo, Chicka Chicka Boom Boom,* and *Red Leaf, Yellow Leaf.*

Lois Ehlert was born on November 9, 1934, in Beaver Dam, Wisconsin. As a child, Lois enjoyed reading. She, her brother, and her sister used to go to the library each week. Each one checked out five books. During the week, they would trade books and read all fifteen.

Art and creativity was encouraged in Lois's family. Her mother gave her scraps of fabric leftover from sewing projects. Her father gave her

---

IN ADDITION TO WRITING AND ILLUSTRATING CHILDREN'S BOOKS, EHLERT HAS ALSO DESIGNED TOYS AND GAMES FOR CHILDREN.

scraps of wood left over from his projects. "I grew up in a home where everyone seemed to be making something with their hands. As far back as I can remember, I was always putting things together, cutting, stitching, pasting, or pounding. The feel of the object I made was as important as the look," remembers Ehlert.

Lois Ehlert continued creating in high school. She went on to study art at the Layton School of Art in Milwaukee, Wisconsin. After graduating in 1957, she got a job as a graphic designer, illustrating children's books. She wasn't very happy with how the children's books looked when they were published and decided not to do that kind of work anymore.

"As I was growing up, I always wanted to be [an] artist. I didn't know what kind of an artist specifically . . . but I knew that's what I wanted to do."

Several years later, Ehlert decided to try illustrating children's books again. This time, she wrote the story, too. Her first try was *Growing Vegetable Soup.* It was a success! Her next book, *Planting a Rainbow,* was also a success. Ehlert had become a full-time author and illustrator.

Details are important to Ehlert. To get the details right, she does lots of research before starting a book. For *Growing Vegetable Soup,* Ehlert looked at pictures in every seed catalog she could find. For *Fish Eyes: A*

THE CAT IN *FEATHERS FOR LUNCH* WAS BASED ON A REAL CAT. EHLERT USED HER NEPHEW'S CAT AS THE MODEL.

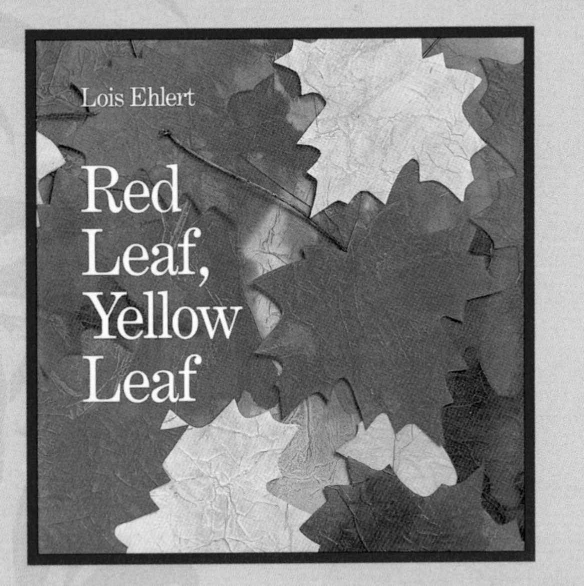

A Selected Bibliography of Ehlert's Work

In My World (2002)
Market Day: A Story Told with Folk Art (2000)
Angel Hide and Seek (Illustrations only, 1998)
Top Cat (1998)
Cuckoo: A Mexican Folktale (1997)
Hands (1997)
Under My Nose (1996)
Snowballs (1995)
Mole's Hill: A Woodland Tale (1994)
Circus (1992)
Red Leaf, Yellow Leaf (1991)
Feathers for Lunch (1990)
Fish Eyes: A Book You Can Count On (1990)
Chicka Chicka Boom Boom (Illustrations only, 1989)
Color Zoo (1989)
Eating the Alphabet: Fruits and Vegetables from A to Z (1989)
Planting a Rainbow (1988)
Growing Vegetable Soup (1987)
Mathematical Games for One or Two (Illustrations only, 1972)

Ehlert's Major Literary Awards

1992 *Boston Globe–Horn Book* Nonfiction Honor Book
Red Leaf, Yellow Leaf

1990 *Boston Globe–Horn Book* Picture Book Honor Book
Chicka Chicka Boom Boom

1990 Caldecott Honor Book
Color Zoo

Book You Can Count On, Ehlert visited the famous Shedd Aquarium in Chicago. For *Eating the Alphabet: Fruits and Vegetables from A to Z,* Ehlert went to the grocery store every week. She bought the vegetables that were in the book so she had them to look at as she did the illustrations.

Ehlert's ideas come from her everyday experiences. "I realize that I write and draw things I know and care about.

"The ideas for my books develop as slowly as seeds I plant in early spring. Ideas and seeds both have to be nurtured to grow. I study, sketch . . . and sit and think."

Yes, a squirrel really did sneak in through my window. Yes, I do enjoy gardening. Yes, I've made snow creatures, and each year I press beautiful maple leaves in my phone books," says Ehlert.

Ehlert has won many awards for her work. She continues to write and illustrate children's picture books.

Where to Find Out More about Lois Ehlert

Books

Kovacs, Deborah, and James Preller. *Meet the Authors and Illustrators: 60 Creators of Favorite Children's Books Talk about Their Work.* Vol. 2. New York: Scholastic, 1991.

Something about the Author. Vol. 69. Detroit: Gale Research, 1992.

Web Sites

Poway Unified School District: Authors Online
http://powayusd.sdcoe.k12.ca.us/pusdtes/Lois%20Ehlert.htm
To read a biographical sketch of Lois Ehlert

Ehlert wears old clothes and a denim apron when she works. She admits she is messy and doesn't clean up every day.

Ed Emberley

Born: October 19, 1931

"I don't really know where I get my ideas. I just tell myself to get an idea and myself does," explains Ed Emberley. Telling himself to get ideas works out very well for Emberley. As the author and illustrator of more than forty books for children, he seems to have plenty of ideas.

Emberley was born in Malden, Massachusetts, on October 19, 1931. One day in first grade, he was drawing a picture of a ship. His teacher came over and watched him draw. She told him what a nice picture it was. Right then, Ed knew he wanted to be an artist.

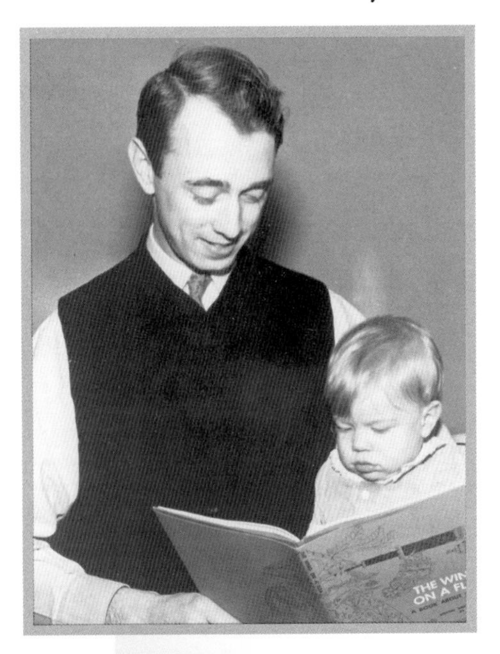

In eighth grade, Ed started taking drawing lessons. He found he enjoyed them more than anything else in school. He continued the lessons in high school.

Later, he went to the Massachusetts School

Ed Emberley's favorite picture book is Beatrix Potter's *The Tale of Peter Rabbit.*

of Art. There he studied painting and illustration—and met his future wife, Barbara. After college, Emberley served two years in the U.S. Army. Then he went back to school and studied art at the Rhode Island School of Design in Providence.

In 1961, Emberley wrote and illustrated his first book, *The Wing on a Flea: A Book about Shapes.* The book showed children how to see shapes in everyday things. He continued to write and illustrate children's books, sometimes working with his wife and children. In 1966,

> *"I expect to be one hundred years old when I retire. If I die first, I'll retire then."*

A Selected Bibliography of Emberley's Work

Thanks, Mom! (2003)
Ed Emberley's Drawing Book of Trucks and Trains (2002)
Ed Emberley's Drawing Book of Weirdos (2001)
Ed Emberley's Fingerprint Drawing Book (2000)
Three: An Emberley Family Sketchbook (1998)
Glad Monster, Sad Monster: A Book about Feelings (1997)
Go Away, Big Green Monster! (1992)
Animals (1987)
Cars, Boats, and Planes (1987)
Home (1987)
Flash, Crash, Rumble, and Roll (Illustrations only, 1985)
Ed Emberley's ABC (1978)
A Birthday Wish (1977)
The Wizard of Op (1975)
Drawing Books: Make a World (1972)
Clothing (Illustrations only, 1969)
Drummer Hoff (Illustrations only, 1967)
Ladybug, Ladybug, Fly Away Home (Illustrations only, 1967)
One Wide River to Cross (Illustrations only, 1966)
The Wing on a Flea: A Book about Shapes (1961)

Emberley's Major Literary Awards

1968 Caldecott Medal
Drummer Hoff

1967 Caldecott Honor Book
One Wide River to Cross

> *"I started drawing the same time most people do—when I was a little child. Most people stop; I didn't."*

Barbara Emberley wrote *One Wide River to Cross,* and Ed illustrated it. Later, Emberley's children, Rebecca and Michael, helped with *Three: An Emberley Family Sketchbook.* Published in 1998, it includes illustrations by Ed Emberley, cutouts by Rebecca Emberley, and comic strip art by Michael Emberley. These days, Emberley's granddaughter helps him with ideas!

Some of Emberley's books use brightly colored woodcuts or clever rhymes to tell a story. Others show young readers how to draw using simple shapes. Some encourage children to come up with new ideas for animals, buildings, and cars. All are illustrated with brilliant colors.

Emberley's drawing books are especially popular. They teach children how to draw everything from grapes to sea monsters. He even has written books showing how to use thumbprints and fingerprints in artwork.

Emberley works on several books at a time and finishes about two books a year. In addition to doing books of his own, he also illustrates books for other people. He has illustrated children's books about computers, science, and the Internet.

EMBERLEY OFTEN ANSWERS HIS READERS' QUESTIONS ABOUT ART VIA E-MAIL. HE EVEN ANSWERS QUESTIONS WHEN HE IS ON VACATION!

His illustrations have won many awards. *One Wide River to Cross* was named a Caldecott Honor Book in 1967. *Drummer Hoff* won a Caldecott Medal in 1968. Barbara Emberley wrote both books.

Ed and Barbara Emberley live in a 300-year-old house in Ipswich, Massachusetts. They enjoy cross-country skiing, sailing, and working on new book ideas together.

Where to Find Out More About Ed Emberley

Books

Kingman, Lee, Grace Allen Hogarth, and Harriet Quimby, comps. *Illustrators of Children's Books, 1967–1976.* Boston: Horn Book, 1978.

Something about the Author. Vol. 8. Detroit: Gale Research, 1976.

Web Sites

Scholastic Authors Online
http://www2.scholastic.com/teachers/authorsandbooks/authorstudies/authorhome.jhtml?authorID=33&collateralID=5156&displayName=Biography
For a biographical sketch of Ed Emberley, a booklist, and an interview with the illustrator

University of Southern Mississippi de Grummond Collection
http://www.lib.usm.edu/~degrum/findaids/emberley.htm
To read a biographical sketch and booklist for Ed Emberley

Ed and Barbara Emberley often print children's books with their own printing press.

Ian Falconer

Born: 1959

Imagine what it's like to write and illustrate your first book. You wonder if anyone will read it and like it. Suddenly, you find that everyone *loves* it!

This is what happened to Ian Falconer. He worked for years as an illustrator, stage set designer, and costume designer. Then he wrote and illustrated a children's book. Almost as soon as his book *Olivia* appeared, it became enormously popular. Teachers, parents, and especially children love the humorous book. *Olivia* was named a Caldecott Honor Book in 2001.

THE DRAWINGS OF OLIVIA ARE DONE IN CHARCOAL.

Falconer originally intended the book to be a Christmas present for his niece Olivia. The little girl, clever and lively, had a big imagination and always managed to charm the grown-ups around her. Falconer started working on a book and chose to depict this Olivia as a feisty little pig!

Falconer illustrated Olivia in black and white with splashes of bright red. He even placed an art lesson in the book. When Olivia visits an art gallery, she gazes at a painting of ballet dancers by Edgar Degas. She also looks with confusion at a modern painting by Jackson Pollock.

"The real Olivia is an extremely headstrong, imaginative child, who even at the age of three (she is seven now), could argue (or stonewall, or bulldoze, or filibuster) through any 'inconvenience' to achieve her goal."

Falconer's second book for children, *Olivia Saves the Circus,* came out in 2001. In this book, the energetic pig claims she became a great circus performer. She says it happened one day when all the circus people came down with ear infections.

Falconer did not start out to produce books. His first love was art. He was born in Ridgefield, Connecticut, in 1959. After high school, he

---

IAN FALCONER HAS CREATED THE ARTWORK FOR MORE THAN A DOZEN COVERS OF *THE NEW YORKER* MAGAZINE.

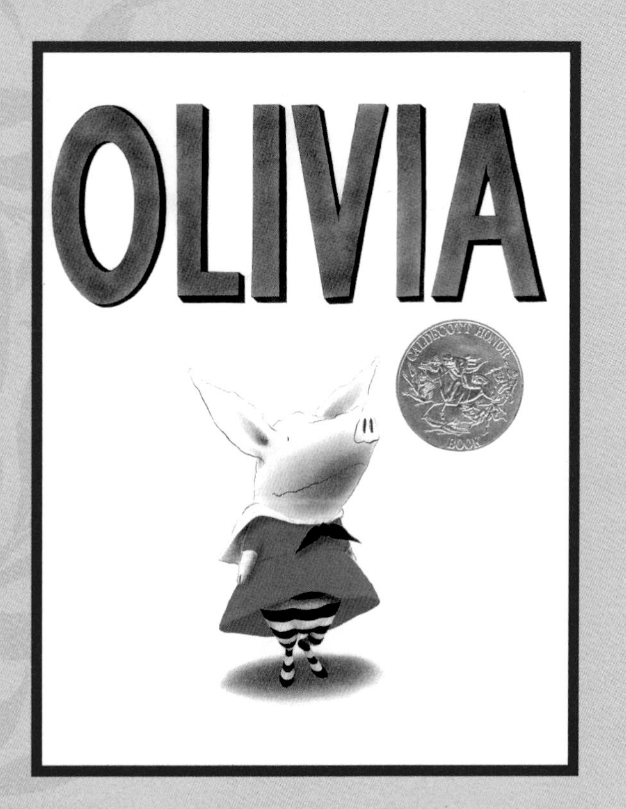

A Selected Bibliography of Falconer's Work

Olivia Saves the Circus (2001)
Olivia (2000)

Falconer's Major Literary Awards

2001 Caldecott Honor Book
Olivia

studied art history at New York University. He also studied painting at the Parsons School of Design in New York City and at the Otis Art Institute in Los Angeles, California.

In the 1980s and 1990s, Falconer worked designing stage sets and costumes for operas and ballets. In 1987, he codesigned costumes for the Los Angeles

"I intended it originally as a little Christmas present for my niece of the same name. . . . At any rate, the drawings and the character [of Olivia] became better and better, so I began to really develop [the book] in earnest."

Opera's production of *Tristan und Isolde,* a tragic story of love and death. Later, he created stage sets and costumes for the Chicago Lyric Opera and costumes for the Royal Opera in London.

Ian Falconer has also designed costumes and sets for the New York City Ballet and the Boston Ballet.

Ian Falconer lives in New York City. He enjoys visiting his niece Olivia—and working on his next book about her pig counterpart!

Where to Find Out More about Ian Falconer

Web Sites

KidsReads.com
http://aol.kidsreads.com/authors/au-falconer-ian.asp
To read a brief biographical sketch of Ian Falconer

Falconer has designed floats that have appeared in the Main Street Parade at Disneyland in California.

Louise Fitzhugh

Born: October 5, 1928
Died: November 19, 1974

Louise Fitzhugh was not afraid to write about controversial subjects. Many people love her frank novels for young readers. But others have banned her book *Harriet the Spy* from some school libraries. They say the idea of spying encourages children to be dishonest and secretive. In *Harriet the Spy,* eleven-year-old Harriet writes about her classmates and neighbors in a secret notebook and then must suffer the consequences when she loses it.

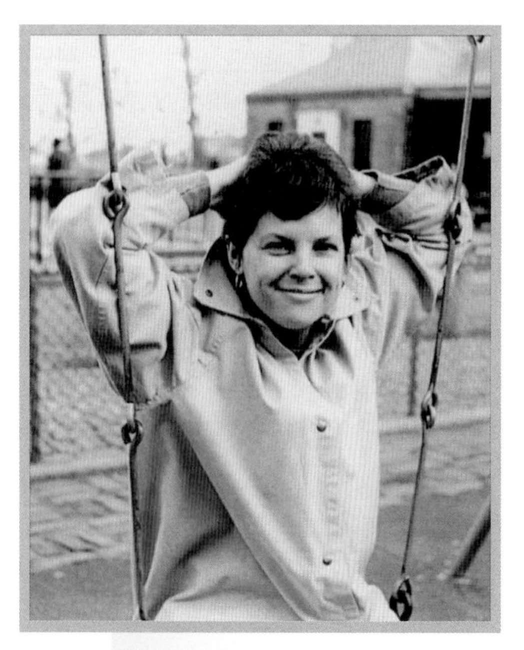

Louise Fitzhugh was born on October 5, 1928, in Memphis, Tennessee. Even though her family was wealthy, Louise did not have a happy childhood. Shortly after Louise was born, her parents were divorced. Both Louise's mother and father wanted custody of their daughter. After a long struggle in a

Harriet the Spy was adapted as a motion picture and released in 1996.

court, her father, a wealthy attorney, received full custody of Louise. She grew up without ever knowing her mother. This caused feelings of loneliness that she later drew on for her books.

Louise enjoyed reading as a young child. She began writing her own stories when she was about eleven years old.

When she finished high school, Louise Fitzhugh wanted to leave the South. She was troubled by the racism and bigotry in Memphis and did not agree with how many people treated African-Americans in the South. She studied literature at three different colleges in Florida and New York. Her interest turned to art, and she left college before earning her degree.

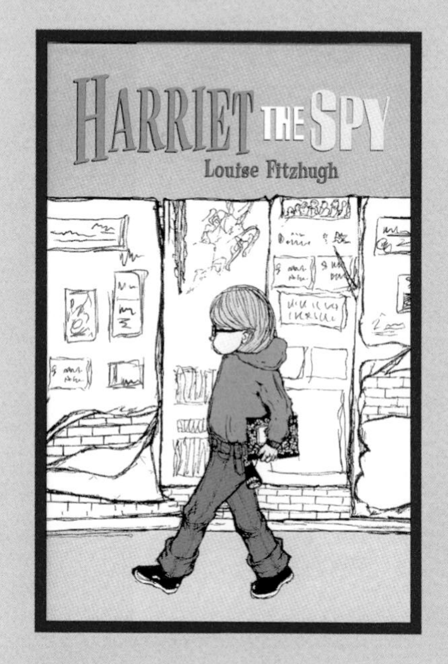

A Selected Bibliography of Fitzhugh's Work

I Am Four (Text only, 1982)
Sport (1979)
I Am Five (1978)
Nobody's Family Is Going to Change (1974)
The Long Secret (1965)
Harriet the Spy (1964)
Suzuki Beane (Illustrations only, 1961)

"Ole Golly says there is as many ways to live as there are people on the earth and I shouldn't go round with blinders but should see every way I can. Then I'll know what way I want to live and not just live like my family."
—*from* Harriet the Spy

Then Fitzhugh studied at two art schools in New York City. She also went to Europe to study art. After returning to New York City, she became a well-respected artist. Many of her oil paintings were exhibited in galleries around the country.

Fitzhugh also continued to write. Much of her writing was in the form of unpublished novels and plays for adults. Her first published children's book was *Suzuki Beane,* which she illustrated for her friend and author Sandra Scoppettone.

"Cook settled herself with a cup of coffee. 'How long you been a spy?' Since I could write. Ole Golly told me if I was going to be a writer I better write down everything, so I'm a spy that writes down everything."
—*from* Harriet the Spy

Fitzhugh continued work on her own book about the independent young Harriet. She had trouble finding a company to publish the novel. Finally, in 1964, *Harriet the Spy* was published.

Fitzhugh's career as a children's author lasted only thirteen years. Louise Fitzhugh died of a burst

---

FITZHUGH'S BOOK *NOBODY'S FAMILY IS GOING TO CHANGE* WAS USED AS THE BASIS FOR THE BROADWAY MUSICAL *THE TAP DANCE KID.*

blood vessel on November 19, 1974, at the age of forty-six. Her third novel, *Nobody's Family Is Going to Change,* was published one week after her death.

Where to Find Out More About Louise Fitzhugh

Books

Collier, Laurie, and Joyce Nakamura, eds. *Authors & Artists for Young Adults.* Vol. 18. Detroit: Gale Research, 1996.

Marcus, Leonard S., ed. *Dear Genius: The Letters of Ursula Nordstrom.* New York: HarperCollins, 1998.

Wolf, Virginia L. *Louise Fitzhugh.* New York: Twayne Publishers, 1991.

Web Sites

Purple Socks: A Louise Fitzhugh Tribute Site
http://www.purple-socks.com/
For a biography of Louise Fitzhugh, a list of her books and characters, and information about Harriet's spy route and where her friends lived

University of North Carolina School of Information and Library Science: Louise Fitzhugh
http://www.ils.unc.edu/~winta/louise/fitzhugh.htm
For a biographical sketch of Louise Fitzhugh, a list of her works, and activities related to *Harriet the Spy*

***Harriet the Spy* has sold more than 2.5 million copies since it was published in 1964.**

Paul Fleischman

Born: September 5, 1952

lthough he is the author of more than twenty books, Paul Fleischman never dreamed he would turn out to be a writer. As a child, he wasn't even much of a reader.

Paul Fleischman was born on September 5, 1952, in Monterey, California, and grew up in Santa Monica. He preferred riding his bike and hanging out on the beach to reading.

Paul's father was a writer, however. Sid Fleischman, who won the Newbery Medal in 1987 for *The Whipping Boy,* often read his unfinished book chapters to his family. Sometimes he asked his wife and children what they thought should happen next. Young Paul loved suggesting ideas to his dad.

WHEN PAUL FLEISCHMAN WAS GROWING UP, THE FAMILY SELDOM WATCHED TELEVISION. THEY PREFERRED READING AND PLAYING MUSIC TOGETHER.

Music was a part of everyday life in the Fleischman home. Paul and his mother played piano, and his father played the guitar. Later in life, Paul Fleischman learned to play the recorder. He also played the accordion and wrote music.

Today, Fleischman is a well-known author of historical novels and poems. Novels give him a chance to do all kinds of historical research. He compares his research to a detective game in which he tracks down unusual bits of information. Fleischman makes sure that his books accurately depict the clothing, language, environment, and ideas of the times in which they are set.

"I never dreamed of becoming a writer. I didn't know what I wanted to be as a child—or a young adult."

Many of his books take place in the eighteenth and nineteenth centuries. They include people from all walks of life—from servants to military leaders to Native Americans. Some of his books tell the story from several different points of view. In *Bull Run,* sixteen people tell their own versions of a Civil War battle. *Saturnalia* is set in 1681 in Boston, Massachusetts. It describes masters, servants, tradesmen, and apprentices.

Fleischman's poetry also has many voices. His books of poetry include *I Am Phoenix: Poems for Two Voices; Joyful Noise: Poems for Two*

THE FLEISCHMAN FAMILY HAD AN OLD-FASHIONED PRINTING PRESS. PAUL AND HIS SISTERS USED IT TO MAKE STATIONERY AND BUSINESS CARDS.

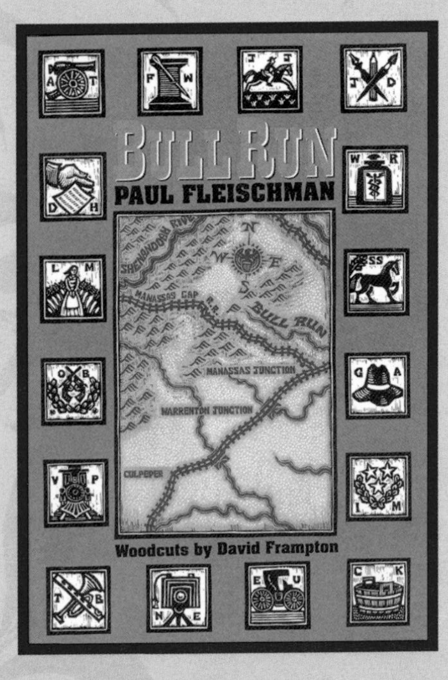

A Selected Bibliography of Fleischman's Work

The Animal Hedge (2003)
Seek (2001)
Big Talk: Poems for Four Voices (2000)
Whirligig (1998)
Seedfolks (1997)
Dateline: Troy (1996)
The Borning Room (1993)
Bull Run (1993)
Saturnalia (1990)
Joyful Noise: Poems for Two Voices (1988)
Coming-and-Going Men: Four Tales (1985)
I Am Phoenix: Poems for Two Voices (1985)
Graven Images: Three Stories (1982)

Fleischman's Major Literary Awards

1994 Scott O'Dell Award
Bull Run

1990 *Boston Globe–Horn Book* Fiction Honor Book
Saturnalia

1989 Newbery Medal
1988 *Boston Globe–Horn Book* Fiction Honor Book
Joyful Noise: Poems for Two Voices

1983 Newbery Honor Book
Graven Images: Three Stories

Voices; and *Big Talk: Poems for Four Voices.* The poems in these collections are meant to be read aloud by several people. Some lines are read by one person alone, and some are read by everyone together, like a choir with solos and harmony singing. It is easy to see that Fleischman's musical background has influenced his writing.

In his book *Seek,* Fleischman builds on the idea of having many voices. *Seek* is the story of Rob, who is looking for

"I do lots of research for my historical novels. It takes many fat books in order to write one thin one."

the father he never knew. Altogether, fifty-two different people enter Rob's story. The story is meant to be read aloud like a play.

Paul Fleischman is married and has two children. He lives in Monterey, California.

Where to Find Out More about Paul Fleischman

Books

McElmeel, Sharron L. *100 Most Popular Children's Authors.* Englewood, Colo.: Libraries Unlimited, 1999.

Pendergast, Tom, and Sara Pendergast, eds. *St. James Guide to Young Adult Writers.* 2nd ed. Detroit: St. James Press, 1999.

Silvey, Anita, ed. *Children's Books and Their Creators.* Boston: Houghton Mifflin, 1995.

Web Sites

Paul Fleischman's Home Page
http://www.paulfleischman.com/
To read a brief biographical sketch of Paul Fleischman and detailed information about his books

TeenReads.com
http://www.teenreads.com/authors/au-fleischman-paul.asp
To read an interview with Paul Fleischman

In recent years, Fleischman has written screenplays for two of his books. He has also written a play called *Zap.*

Sid Fleischman

Born: March 16, 1920

Before he became a Newbery Medal–winning author, Sid Fleischman entertained people as a professional magician! He traveled around the country entertaining people with his magic. Though his days as a magician are behind him, he still entertains people—with his books.

Fleischman has written novels and screenplays for adults. He is best known as the author of the Josh McBroom series, the Bloodhound Gang series, and *The Whipping Boy,* a story about the adventures of a royal prince and an orphan boy who receives a whipping whenever the young prince does something wrong.

Albert Sidney Fleischman was born on March 16, 1920, in Brooklyn, New York. He grew up in San Diego, California. As a young

IN 1987, FLEISCHMAN WON THE NEWBERY MEDAL FOR *THE WHIPPING BOY.* TWO YEARS LATER, HIS SON, PAUL FLEISCHMAN, WON THE SAME AWARD FOR HIS BOOK, *JOYFUL NOISE: POEMS FOR TWO VOICES.*

boy, Sid was interested in storytelling, but he did not think about being a writer. He wanted to be a magician, so he read as many books as he could about magic tricks. Sid practiced tricks and even invented some tricks of his own.

Sid Fleischman decided to write a book that included some of his magic tricks. *Between Cocktails* was published when he

> *"I suspect my magician's mind reveals itself in the way I plot my scenes and write my characters. I cannot resist mystery, surprise, and heroes capable of a kind of sleight-of-mind in outwitting the villains."*

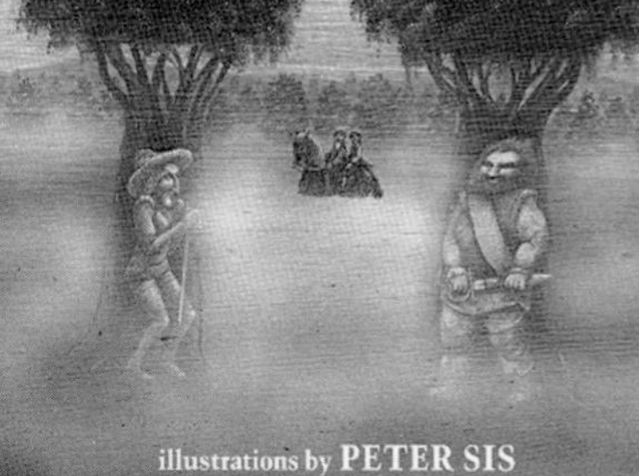

A Selected Bibliography of Fleischman's Work

Bo & Mzzz Mad (2001)
A Carnival of Animals (2000)
McBroom Tells a Lie (1999)
Bandit's Moon (1998)
Chancy and the Grand Rascal (1997)
The Abracadabra Kid: A Writer's Life (1996)
13th Floor: A Ghost Story (1995)
Here Comes McBroom: Three More Tall Tales (1992)
The Midnight Horse (1990)
The Scarebird (1988)
The Whipping Boy (1986)
McBroom Tells the Truth (1981)
Humbug Mountain (1978)
McBroom and the Beanstalk (1978)
Jingo Django (1971)
Longbeard the Wizard (1970)
The Ghost in the Noonday Sun (1965)
By the Great Horn Spoon! (1963)
Mr. Mysterious & Company (1962)

Fleischman's Major Literary Awards

1987 Newbery Medal
The Whipping Boy

1979 *Boston Globe–Horn Book* Fiction Award
Humbug Mountain

was just seventeen years old! "When I saw my name on the cover, I was hooked on writing books," Fleischman says.

After he finished high school, Sid Fleischman traveled around the country entertaining people with his magic act. He heard many stories and folktales from people he met in small towns. Many of these stories later influenced his writing. He served in the U.S. Naval Reserve during World War II (1939–1945). When he left the military in 1945, he took a job at a newspaper in San Diego.

> *"The books we enjoy as children stay with us forever—they have a special impact. Paragraph after paragraph, and page after page, the author must deliver his or her best work."*

In 1951, Fleischman began his career as a full-time writer. He started out writing for adults. His own children did not understand what he did for a living. "I decided to clear up the mystery and wrote a book just for them," Fleischman explains. He wanted his children to know that he earned money by writing. The story that Fleischman wrote for his children became *Mr. Mysterious & Company.* His first children's book, it was published in 1962.

An important part of Fleischman's writing for children is humor. He is also known for using crazy names for characters in his books. "I collect interesting names, funny names and outrageous names, and some-

It took Fleischman almost ten years to write *The Whipping Boy.* He thought of the idea for the book while doing research for another book.

times the name itself helps me to create a character," he explains.

Fleischman lives near the Pacific Ocean in Santa Monica, California. He has written more than fifty books for young people and adults.

Where to Find Out More about Sid Fleischman

Books

Berger, Laura Stanley, ed. *Twentieth Century Children's Writers.* Detroit: St. James Press, 1995.

Cart, Michael. *What's So Funny: Wit and Humor in American Children's Literature.* New York: HarperCollins, 1995.

Fleischman, Sid. *The Abracadabra Kid: A Writer's Life.* New York: Greenwillow Books, 1996.

Kovacs, Deborah, and James Preller. *Meet the Authors and Illustrators: 60 Creators of Famous Children's Books Talk about Their Work.* Vol. 2. New York: Scholastic, 1991.

Web Sites

Educational Paperback Association
http://www.edupaperback.org/authorbios/Fleischman_Sid.html
To read an autobiographical sketch and booklist for Sid Fleischman

Random House: Sid Fleischman
http://www.randomhouse.com/teachers/authors/flei.html
To find out about Sid Fleischman's favorite books, hobbies, and foods

Fleischman's *By the Great Horn Spoon!* was adapted into the 1967 movie called *The Adventures of Bullwhip Griffin.* His book *The Ghost in the Noonday Sun* was also made into a movie, which was released in 1974.

Denise Fleming

Born: January 31, 1950

Most people imagine an artist as someone working with pencils or paintbrushes. But Denise Fleming is different. She starts her art projects with tubs of soft, colored mush. Fleming uses the mush to make her own paper. When she's finished, she has thick, wet sheets with the images set right in.

Denise Fleming was born on January 31, 1950, in Toledo, Ohio. As a child, she and her younger sister liked to spend their free time outdoors. They rode bikes, ran races, and put on plays for their friends. In school, Denise especially liked art classes. When she was only a third-grader, she was chosen to take art classes at the local art museum. One of

---

Fleming's husband, David, and daughter, Indigo, help in the papermaking process. David makes the stencils and all three discuss picture ideas for books.

her paintings received a special honor. It was picked to be on the cover of a teachers' magazine!

Denise Fleming's parents were also creative. Her father had a workshop in the basement where he built furniture. Her mother was active in the local theater. Both parents encouraged Denise's creativity and artwork. Denise loved to spend hours in the basement while her dad worked on furniture. She would find her own space and make things out of papier-mâché and wood.

"The whole process [of papermaking] is wet, messy, and wonderful."

In high school, Denise took art classes and won several art awards. Then she moved to Michigan and went to Kendall College of Art and Design. In college, she met another artist named David Powers. Powers and Fleming got married after college and went to work.

For a while, Fleming illustrated children's books written by other people. In time, she decided she would rather work on her own projects. She quit her job, and she and her husband delved into different kinds of art, carpentry, and furniture building.

Then Fleming and her sister took a class in papermaking. They learned about making pulp and how to turn it into paper. Fleming loved the class and took another one. Soon she began experimenting on her own. She enjoyed sinking her hands into the thick, wet pulp, mixing

---

DENISE FLEMING TOOK AN ART CLASS AT A MUSEUM IN THE THIRD GRADE. SOME OF HER PICTURES WERE PICKED TO BE IN AN ART EXCHANGE PROGRAM WITH OTHER COUNTRIES.

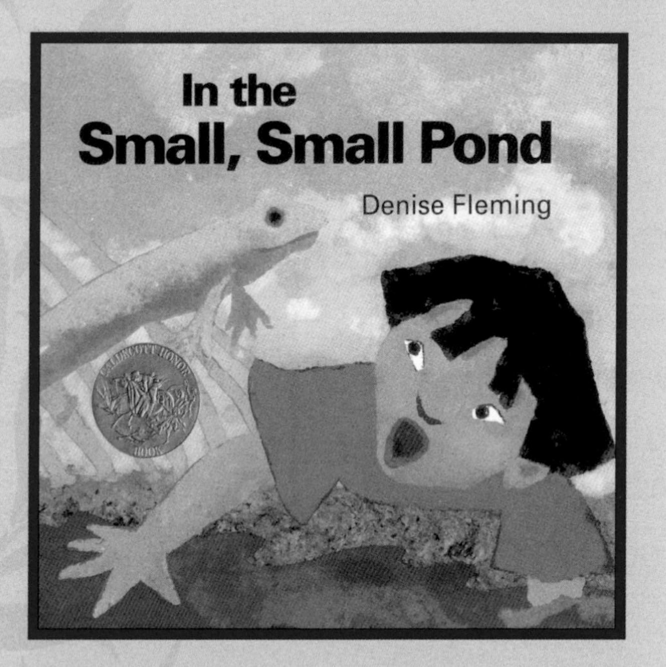

A Selected Bibliography of Fleming's Work

Alphabet under Construction (2002)
Pumpkin Eye (2001)
The Everything Book (2000)
Mama Cat Has Three Kittens (1998)
Time to Sleep (1997)
Where Once There Was a Wood (1996)
Barnyard Banter (1994)
In the Small, Small Pond (1993)
Count! (1992)
Lunch (1992)
In the Tall, Tall Grass (1991)

Fleming's Major Literary Awards

1994 Caldecott Honor Book
In the Small, Small Pond

1992 *Boston Globe–Horn Book* Picture Book Award
In the Tall, Tall Grass

colors into it, and seeing how the colors and fibers blended.

Fleming developed a way of making pictures by pushing colored pulp through stencils. The result is a rich, colorful image built right into the paper. Sometimes the pulp seems to have a mind of its own. In the finished artwork, some areas of color have sharp, clear edges. Other areas have soft edges where colors have seeped into each other. Some colors are strong and solid. Others are mottled or speckled.

Fleming calls her works "pulp paintings." She used them to illustrate her 1991 book for small children, *In the Tall, Tall, Grass.* The book is full of short rhymes and colorful close-ups of animals. In 1993, she wrote *In the Small, Small Pond* and again used pulp paintings. This book was named a Caldecott Honor Book for its splendid illustrations.

> *"I haven't picked up a brush or a colored pencil since I discovered papermaking."*

Today, Denise Fleming continues to write and illustrate books for young children. She lives in Toledo, Ohio, with her husband, their daughter, Indigo, and many, many cats.

Where to Find Out More about Denise Fleming

Books

Holtze, Sally Holmes, ed. *Seventh Book of Junior Authors & Illustrators.* New York: H. W. Wilson Company, 1996.

Something about the Author. Vol. 126. Detroit: Gale Research, 2002.

Web Sites

KidsReads.com
http://www.kidsreads.com/authors/au-fleming-denise.asp
To read a short biography of Fleming and some fun facts about her

Online Home of Children's Author/Illustrator Denise Fleming
http://denisefleming.com/
To visit Fleming's Web site and download her papermaking and bookbinding instructions

---

Fleming's book *Mama Cat Has Three Kittens* is dedicated to Abigail, the first cat she had as a child.

Esther Forbes

Born: June 28, 1891
Died: August 12, 1967

A passion for history ran in Esther Forbes's family. Forbes's mother had an attic full of old books about New England history. As a child, Esther Forbes loved to page through the history books. In fact, the Forbes family was itself a part of New England history. In the 1600s, one of Esther Forbes's ancestors was accused of being a witch. She died in jail.

Esther Forbes used her passion for New England history to write biographies and historical novels. She was born on June 28, 1891, in Westborough, Massachusetts. Her father, William Trowbridge Forbes, was a judge. Her mother, Harriet Merrifield Forbes, was a writer and local historian. Forbes attended Bradford Academy

---

DURING WORLD WAR I (1914–1918), ESTHER FORBES LEFT COLLEGE TO WORK ON A FARM IN WEST VIRGINIA. THE CROPS GROWN THERE SUPPORTED THE U.S. WAR EFFORT.

and the University of Wisconsin.

In 1920, Forbes began working as an editor at the Houghton Mifflin publishing company. She also began working on her own writing. In 1926, she published her first novel for adult readers, called

> *"Already on every village green throughout New England, men and boys were drilling in defiance of the King's orders. They said they were afraid of an attack from the French. These men had no uniforms. They came from the fields and farms in the very clothes they used for plowing."*—from Johnny Tremain

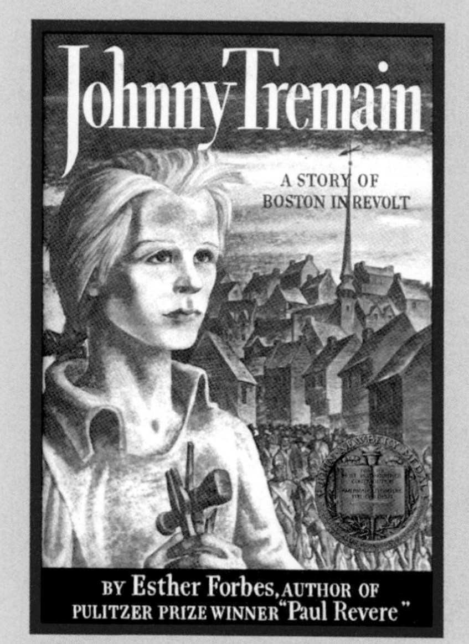

A Selected Bibliography of Forbes's Work

America's Paul Revere (1946)

Johnny Tremain (1943)

Forbes's Major Literary Awards

1944 Newbery Medal
Johnny Tremain

> *"His hand came down on top of the furnace. The burn was so terrible he at first felt no pain, but stood stupidly looking at his hand. For one second, before the metal cooled, the inside of his right hand, from wrist to fingertips, was coated with solid silver."*
> —*from* Johnny Tremain

O Genteel Lady! She published five more novels in the next twelve years. One of them, *A Mirror for Witches,* was based on the story of her ancestor who had been charged with witchcraft.

In 1943, Esther Forbes published a biography of the patriot Paul Revere. *Paul Revere and the World He Lived In* describes Revere's life as well as everyday life in Boston in the 1700s. Forbes's mother helped her research the book, which won the 1943 Pulitzer Prize for history.

Forbes and her mother gathered so much interesting research that Forbes decided to write another book. *Johnny Tremain* is set in Boston at the beginning of the American Revolution. The title character is a silversmith's apprentice. (A silversmith makes objects of silver. An apprentice is a worker learning a trade from a master craftsman.) *Johnny Tremain,* the only novel Forbes wrote for young readers, became her best-known work.

In the book, Johnny Tremain becomes involved with a group of patriots fighting against the British after an accident prevents him from becoming a silversmith. The story puts Tremain in the midst of many

ESTHER FORBES ONCE SAID THAT SHE HOPED *JOHNNY TREMAIN* WOULD "SHOW THE BOYS AND GIRLS OF TODAY HOW DIFFICULT WERE THOSE OTHER CHILDREN'S LIVES BY MODERN STANDARDS."

real historic events, including the Boston Tea Party. As a messenger for the American patriots, Tremain meets John Hancock, Samuel Adams, and other patriots. Paul Revere also appears as a character in the book. In the process of helping win American independence from Britain, Tremain begins to grow to manhood.

Like *Paul Revere and the World He Lived In, Johnny Tremain* won high praise from critics and readers. The book won the 1944 Newbery Medal. *Johnny Tremain* is today considered a classic of children's literature. In 1946, Esther Forbes wrote another book about Paul Revere. Called *America's Paul Revere,* this biography was also for young readers. Esther Forbes died on August 12, 1967, at the age of seventy-six.

WHERE TO FIND OUT MORE ABOUT ESTHER FORBES

BOOKS

Sutherland, Zena. *Children & Books.* 9th ed. New York: Addison Wesley Longman, 1997.

Vollstadt, Elizabeth Weiss. *Understanding Johnny Tremain.* San Diego: Lucent Books, 2001.

WEB SITES

EDUCATIONAL PAPERBACK ASSOCIATION
http://www.edupaperback.org/authorbios/Forbes_Esther.html
To read a biographical sketch and booklist for Esther Forbes

FUN TRIVIA QUIZ
http://www.funtrivia.com/dir/4515.html
To take a Johnny Tremain quiz created by young fans

A MOVIE VERSION OF *JOHNNY TREMAIN* WAS RELEASED IN 1957.

Mem Fox

Born: March 5, 1946

em Fox has lived in many countries throughout the world. But as an adult, she returned to her native Australia. Many of her picture books for children show life in Australia. Her books also include themes about the importance of a strong family. Her more than thirty books for children have been published in many languages, including Indonesian, Chinese, Japanese, German, and Hebrew. Her best-known books include *Time for Bed, Hattie and the Fox, Koala Lou,* and *Night Noises.*

Mem Fox was born on March 5, 1946, in Melbourne, Australia. When she was only six months old, her family moved to the African

Mem Fox's real name is Merrion Frances Fox.

nation of Zimbabwe. Her missionary father had been sent to work in Africa. When she was old enough to go to school, Mem attended the mission school. She was the only white student there. After a year, she left to attend an all-white school in a nearby village.

Mem did not like how black people were treated in Africa. There was a great deal of racism in Zimbabwe and throughout Africa. When she finished high school, she decided to leave Africa. She moved to London, England, to attend Rose Bruford College, where she studied drama. Life in London was very different from what she was used to in Africa. She spent four years in London before graduating from college in 1968.

"I write for the child-within-the parent who is reading to the child. I always write with adult readers in mind because my audience is often too young to read on their own."

She married Malcolm Fox in 1969, and they lived in Africa briefly before moving to Australia in 1970. She taught drama at a college in Adelaide, Australia. During her career as a teacher, Fox also taught at other colleges and universities in Australia. She also went back to college in Australia to study children's literature.

As an assignment for one of her children's literature classes, she

FOX'S BOOK *TIME FOR BED* WAS NAMED TO OPRAH WINFREY'S LIST OF THE TWENTY ALL-TIME BEST CHILDREN'S BOOKS.

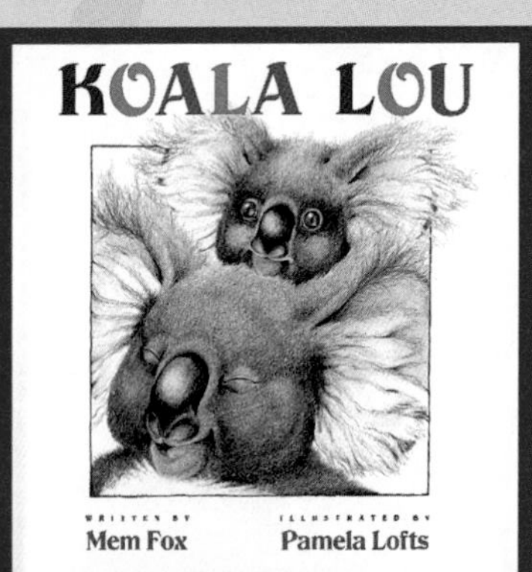

A Selected Bibliography of Fox's Work

The Magic Hat (2002)
Harriet, You'll Drive Me Wild (2000)
Sleepy Bears (1999)
Because of the Bloomers (1998)
Whoever You Are (1997)
A Bedtime Story (1996)
Feathers and Fools (1996)
Sophie (1994)
Time for Bed (1993)
Guess What? (1990)
Night Noises (1989)
Shoes from Grandpa (1989)
Koala Lou (1988)
With Love, at Christmas (1988)
Hattie and the Fox (1987)
Arabella: The Smallest Girl in the World (1986)
Wilfrid Gordon McDonald Partridge (1984)
Possum Magic (1983)

wrote the draft of her first book, *Possum Magic.* She tried to get the book published, but it was rejected nine times in five years. She finally found a publisher who liked the book. Published in 1983, *Possum Magic* sold more than one million copies in its first ten years of publication. It is Australia's best-selling picture book.

Along with her writing and teaching, Fox has worked on literacy, or teaching people to

"A five-hundred word book takes me around two years to perfect. Only the best is good enough for kids. Only the best pays my mortgage."

read. She has traveled all around the world giving speeches and workshops on literacy. She has received many awards for her work as a language arts expert as well as for her writing.

Mem Fox is retired from teaching, but she still travels as a literacy expert. She lives with her husband in Adelaide, Australia. She continues to write picture books for children.

Where to Find Out More About Mem Fox

Books

Fox, Mem. *Dear Mem Fox, I Have Read All Your Books, Even the Pathetic Ones: And Other Incidents in the Life of a Children's Book Author.* San Diego: Harcourt Brace Jovanovich, 1992.

Mem's the Word. New York: Penguin, 1990.

Kovacs, Deborah, and James Preller. *Meet the Authors and Illustrators: 60 Creators of Favorite Children's Books Talk about Their Work.* Vol. 2. New York: Scholastic, 1993.

Web Sites

Mem Fox Home Page
http://www.memfox.net/
To read an autobiographical sketch by Mem Fox and information about her books

Pan Macmillan: Australia Online
http://www.panmacmillan.com.au/pandemonium/mem.htm
To read a biographical sketch of Mem Fox and lists of things that she loves and loathes

---

Mem Fox's father's name, Wilfrid Gordon McDonald Partridge, is also the title of her second book. In the same book, there is a character named Miss Nancy—Fox's mother's name!

Paula Fox

Born: April 22, 1923

Most writers will tell you that using your own life experiences to gather ideas for books is the best way to develop interesting stories. In the case of author Paula Fox, her life experiences have been so varied that it's no wonder she writes books full of truth and richness for adults and young readers.

Paula Fox was born on April 22, 1923, in New York City. Paula's parents were more interested in their world travels than in being parents. After Paula was born, her father, a writer, and her mother left her at an orphanage. Although Paula did see her parents again, her contact with them was always brief.

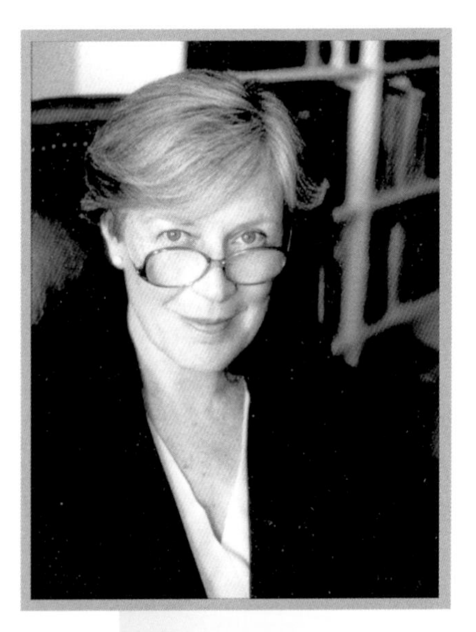

Paula spent her early years living with a minister, whom she called Uncle Elwood, and his family in upstate New York. Uncle Elwood taught Paula to read and introduced her to libraries. The young girl

It took Paula Fox three months to write the first ten pages of *Borrowed Finery: A Memoir.* She used to write an entire novel for young readers in that time.

was instantly spellbound by books. “Libraries meant freedom, solace, and truth to me,” she says now. “Stories took me to other places. There was no television then, of course. Reading was everything to me.”

Books and stories grounded Paula during the years she moved from place to place. At the age of six, Paula went to live with her grandmother in New York City. Her grandmother told stories of her youth in Spain. “Some of her tales were comic,” Fox recalls, “and some were tales of dread.”

The following year, Paula

> *“A lie hides the truth. A story tries to find it.”*

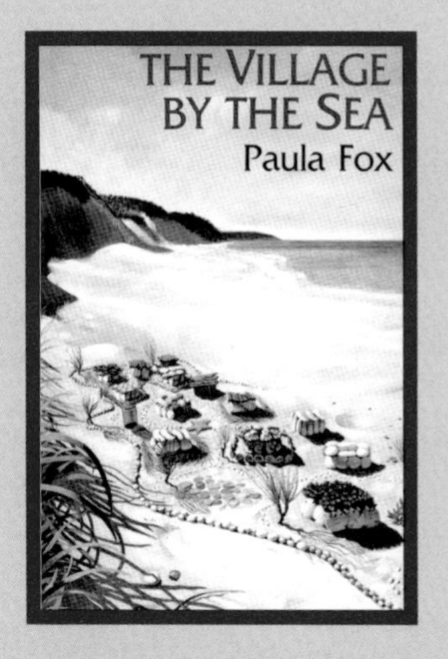

A Selected Bibliography of Fox's Work

Radiance Descending (1997)
The Eagle Kite (1995)
Western Wind (1993)
Monkey Island (1991)
The Village by the Sea (1988)
One-Eyed Cat (1984)
A Place Apart (1980)
The Slave Dancer (1973)
Blowfish Live in the Sea (1970)
Portrait of Ivan (1969)
The Stone-Faced Boy (1968)
How Many Miles to Babylon? (1967)
Maurice's Room (1966)

Fox's Major Literary Awards

1994 *Boston Globe–Horn Book* Fiction Honor Book
Western Wind

1989 *Boston Globe–Horn Book* Fiction Award
The Village by the Sea

1985 Newbery Honor Book
One-Eyed Cat

1983 National Book Award
A Place Apart

1978 Hans Christian Andersen Medal for Authors

1974 Newbery Medal
The Slave Dancer

"No one can really explain what it is that drives them to write. It is simply a need. One of the nicest things about writing is that you make yourself laugh. You don't have to wait for a comedian to come along!"

joined her parents in California, but by the age of eight, she was separated from them again. She was sent to Cuba to live on a sugar plantation with relatives. Because she attended many schools in many different places, the library became the one constant in Paula's life.

By the age of sixteen, Paula Fox began working. Her first job was at the Warner Brothers movie studio in Hollywood, where she read novels written in English or Spanish to see if they would make good films. She later worked as a teacher, a salesperson, a model, and a lathe operator.

Paula Fox's first novel, *Poor George,* is for adults. It was published in 1967. She soon followed with a second novel called *Desperate Characters,* which was made into a movie in 1971.

Recalling her love of books as a child, Fox decided to try her hand at writing for young readers. Her first book for children was *Maurice's Room.* In 1973, she wrote *The Slave Dancer,* a historical novel about a boy who is kidnapped and put on a slave ship—and it won a Newbery Medal! Her other popular books for young readers include *Blowfish Live in the Sea; A Place Apart;* and *One-Eyed Cat.*

BECAUSE PAULA FOX MOVED A LOT AS A CHILD, BY THE TIME SHE WAS TWELVE YEARS OLD SHE HAD ATTENDED NINE DIFFERENT SCHOOLS!

At the age of seventy-six, Fox was attacked while strolling with her husband during a visit to Israel. She suffered head injuries and slight brain damage. After two years of therapy, during which time she struggled to regain her grasp of language, Paula Fox began writing again. The writing became an important part of her recovery, as a way back to normal life.

The result of this work is her memoir for adults, *Borrowed Finery: A Memoir,* in which she recounts the details of her amazing life. Fortunately, readers now get a chance to learn the true story of a writer whose real life is as interesting as any fiction she ever wrote.

Where to Find Out More about Paula Fox

Books

Drew, Bernard A. *The 100 Most Popular Young Adult Authors.* Englewood, Colo.: Libraries Unlimited, 1996.

Fox, Paula. *Borrowed Finery: A Memoir.* New York: Henry Holt, 2001.

Silvey, Anita, ed. *Children's Books and Their Creators.* Boston: Houghton Mifflin, 1995

Sutherland, Zena. *Children & Books.* 9th ed. New York: Addison Wesley Longman, 1997.

Web Sites

RANDOM HOUSE: AUTHORS/ILLUSTRATORS
http://www.randomhouse.com/teachers/authors/pfox.html
To read an autobiographical sketch and booklist for Paula Fox

PAULA FOX BECAME FLUENT IN SPANISH DURING THE YEARS SHE ATTENDED A ONE-ROOM SCHOOLHOUSE WHILE LIVING ON A SUGAR PLANTATION IN CUBA.

Russell Freedman

Born: October 11, 1929

A newspaper article launched Russell Freedman on a career of writing books for young people. One day, while he was reading the *New York Times,* he noticed a story about a blind sixteen-year-old boy who had invented a Braille typewriter. (Braille is a system of printing for the blind. It uses raised dots that are "read" with the fingertips.) Freedman learned another interesting fact: almost 100 years ago, it was another blind sixteen-year-old, Louis Braille, who invented Braille.

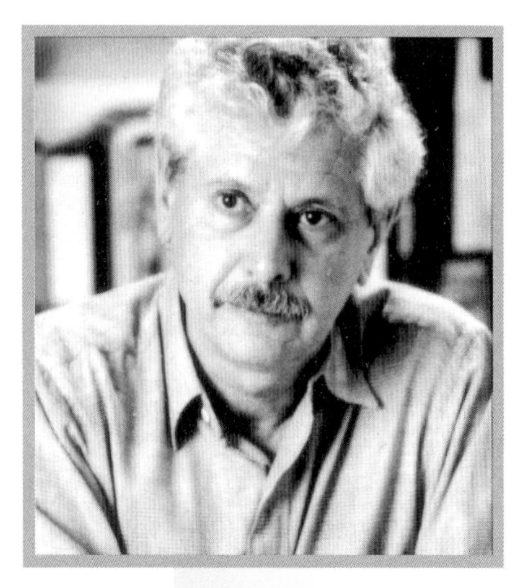

Soon Freedman was at work on *Teenagers Who Made History.* The book, published in 1961, told the story of young people who achieved great things. Freedman had discovered his vocation and has since written more than forty nonfiction books for children.

Freedman was born on October 11, 1929, in San Francisco, California. Books were important part of his family life. His father was West Coast sales

---

Russell Freedman's *Lincoln: A Photobiography* was the first nonfiction book to win the Newbery Medal in thirty-two years.

manager for a big publisher, and many famous authors came to dinner at his house.

"I don't know if I would ever want to write about someone I didn't admire. Writing a biography takes a year of my life. It means in a sense that I live with that person for a year."

After graduating from college in 1951, Freedman joined the U.S. Army and fought in the Korean War. When he returned home, he became a newspaper reporter. He also worked in public relations before turning to book writing.

Many of Freedman's first books were about animals. He discovered that photographs made his books stronger and clearer. So he learned how to research photos, sifting through as many as 1,000 pictures to find just the ones he wanted. He taught himself to write and plan books so that words and pictures worked together.

Then in 1980, he went to an exhibit of photographs of street children from the late nineteenth century. "What impressed me most of all was the way that those old photographs seemed to defy the passage of time," Freedman says. He took his editor to see the show. The result was *Immigrant Kids,* the first book in a new series of histories and biographies that Freedman wrote in the 1980s and 1990s.

Russell Freedman has written books about children in the Wild

---

RUSSELL FREEDMAN DOESN'T LIKE TO BE CALLED A "NONFICTION WRITER." HE BELIEVES MANY PEOPLE THINK NONFICTION ISN'T AS IMPORTANT OR INTERESTING AS FICTION. FREEDMAN PREFERS TO BE CALLED A "FACTUAL AUTHOR."

A Selected Bibliography of Freedman's Work

Confucius: The Golden Rule (2002)
In the Days of the Vaqueros: America's First True Cowboys (2001)
Give Me Liberty!: The Story of the Declaration of Independence (2000)
Babe Didrikson Zaharias: The Making of a Champion (1999)
Martha Graham, a Dancer's Life (1998)
Out of Darkness: The Story of Louis Braille (1997)
The Life and Death of Crazy Horse (1996)
Kids at Work: Lewis Hine and the Crusade against Child Labor (1994)
Eleanor Roosevelt: A Life of Discovery (1993)
An Indian Winter (1992)
The Wright Brothers: How They Invented the Airplane (1991)
Franklin Delano Roosevelt (1990)
Buffalo Hunt (1988)
Indian Chiefs (1987)
Lincoln: A Photobiography (1987)
Cowboys of the Wild West (1985)
Children of the Wild West (1983)
Immigrant Kids (1980)
Teenagers Who Made History (1961)

Freedman's Major Literary Awards

1998 *Boston Globe–Horn Book* Nonfiction Honor Book
Martha Graham, a Dancer's Life

1998 Laura Ingalls Wilder Award

1997 Carter G. Woodson Honor Book
1997 Orbis Pictus Honor Book
The Life and Death of Crazy Horse

1995 Orbis Pictus Honor Book
Kids at Work: Lewis Hine and the Crusade against Child Labor

1994 *Boston Globe–Horn Book* Nonfiction Award
1994 Newbery Honor Book
Eleanor Roosevelt: A Life of Discovery

1992 Newbery Honor Book
1991 *Boston Globe–Horn Book* Nonfiction Honor Book
The Wright Brothers: How They Invented the Airplane

1991 Orbus Pictus Award
Franklin Delano Roosevelt

1989 Carter G. Woodson Outstanding Merit Book
Buffalo Hunt

1988 Newbery Medal
Lincoln: A Photobiography

1984 *Boston Globe–Horn Book* Nonfiction Honor Book
Children of the Wild West

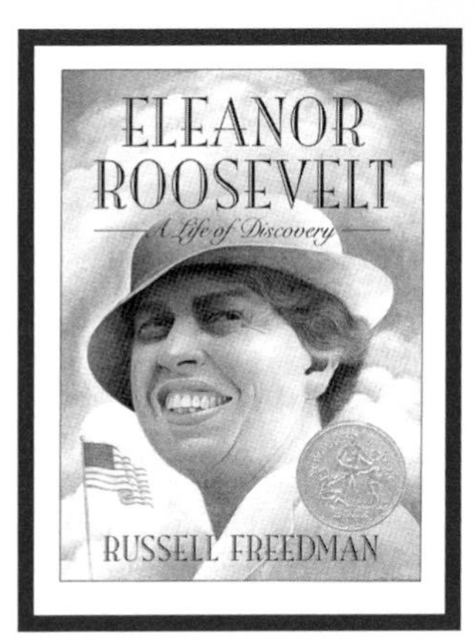

West, cowboys, and Indian chiefs. All of them are illustrated with historical photos and show readers what life was really like for people in the past.

In time, Freedman turned his attention to individual people, creating a kind of book he called "photobiography." His best-known photobiography is of U.S. president Abraham Lincoln. To write it, Freedman studied letters Lincoln had written and received and pored over historical photos. He visited places where Lincoln had lived—and the place where he died.

More photobiographies followed. Freedman feels the people he writes about have messages for readers about how to live life. "If you want to know who my heroes are, take a look at my books. I was drawn to Eleanor Roosevelt because of the quality of her heart; to Crazy Horse because of his courage and his uncompromising integrity; to Abraham Lincoln because of his spirit of forgiveness," Freedman says.

"Isn't it more encouraging for a young reader to know that others, even the great figures of history, have shared the doubts and fears a child feels, than to be confronted with a paragon?"

Where to Find Out More About Russell Freedman

Books

Kovacs, Deborah, and James Preller. *Meet the Authors and Illustrators: 60 Creators of Favorite Children's Books Talk about Their Work.* Vol. 2. New York: Scholastic, 1993.

McElmeel, Sharron L. *100 Most Popular Children's Authors.* Englewood, Colo.: Libraries Unlimited, 1999.

Web Sites

HOUGHTON MIFFLIN: MEET THE AUTHOR
http://www.eduplace.com/kids/hmr/mtai/freedman.html
To read a biographical sketch and booklist for Russell Freedman

---

ONE OF FREEDMAN'S FAVORITE BOOKS, HENDRIK WILLEM VAN LOON'S *THE STORY OF MANKIND,* WON THE VERY FIRST NEWBERY MEDAL. "I THINK IT WAS THE FIRST BOOK THAT GAVE ME A SENSE OF HISTORY AS A LIVING THING," FREEDMAN SAYS.

Don Freeman

Born: August 11, 1908
Died: February 1, 1978

As a little boy, Don Freeman loved to draw. But his career as an artist almost never happened. In fact, Freeman's first job was as a trumpet player!

Don Freeman was born on August 11, 1908, in San Diego, California. Because his parents were not able to care for their children, Don and his older brother, Warren, lived with a guardian named Mrs. Blass in Chula Vista, about 11 miles away from San Diego. Don Freeman's father remained in San Diego, where he worked in a clothing store. He visited his sons every Sunday and often brought Don art materials.

CORDUROY HAS APPEARED IN AN ANIMATED TELEVISION SERIES AND SEVERAL VIDEOS.

A few years later, the Freeman boys were able to join their father in San Diego. Mrs. Blass came along to care for Don and Warren. Don spent many hours in the clothing store where his father worked. He enjoyed sketching the customers. In the evening, Don and his father often went to the theater. Don Freeman also loved music. For his tenth birthday, his father gave him a trumpet. Don taught himself to play by listening to records.

After he graduated from high school, Freeman took art

> *"Creating picture books for children fulfills all my enthusiasms and interests and love of life."*

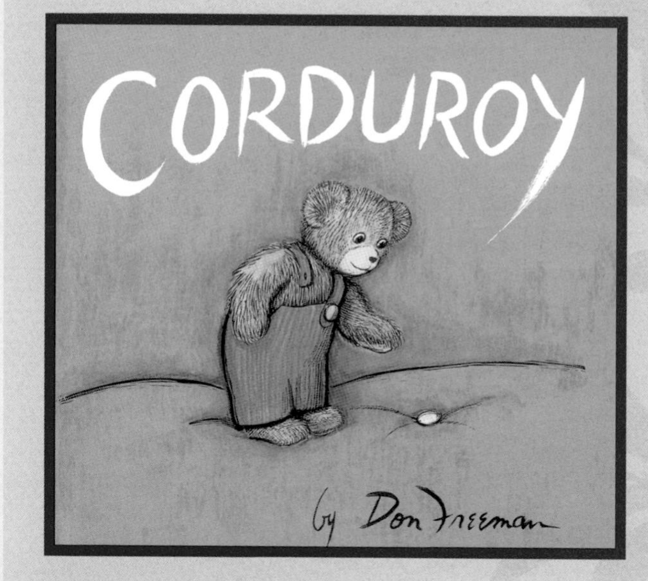

A Selected Bibliography of Freeman's Work

A Pocket for Corduroy (1978)
Bearymore (1976)
The Paper Party: Story and Pictures (1974)
Tilly Witch (1969)
Corduroy (1968)
Best Friends (Illustrations only, 1967)
Dandelion (1964)
Norman the Doorman (1959)
Space Witch (1959)
Fly High, Fly Low (1957)
Ghost Town Treasure (Illustrations only, 1957)
Mop Top (1955)
Beady Bear: Story and Pictures (1954)
Pet of the Met (1953)
Chuggy and the Blue Caboose (1951)

Freeman's Major Literary Awards

1958 Caldecott Honor Book
Fly High, Fly Low

classes at the San Diego School of Fine Arts. In 1929, he hitchhiked across the country to New York City. To support himself, he played the trumpet that his father had given him years before. Freeman also studied at New York's Art Students League and spent hours walking around the city and sketching the people and things he saw.

In 1930, Freeman's musical career ended when he accidentally left his trumpet on the subway. Freeman began drawing for several New York City newspapers and magazines. In 1931, he married Lydia Cooley, an artist he had met at the San Diego School of Fine Arts. The couple later had a son named Roy Warren.

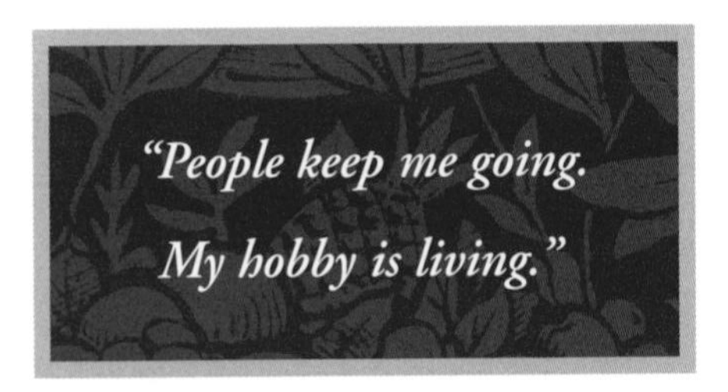

During the 1940s, Freeman illustrated several books for adults. He also published *It Shouldn't Happen,* a book of cartoons based on his experiences in the U.S. Army. In 1949, the Freeman family moved to Santa Barbara, California. Then Freeman and his wife wrote and illustrated their first children's book, *Chuggy and the Blue Caboose,* which was published in 1951.

After creating Chuggy, Freeman focused on writing and illustrating books for children. His second book, *Pet of the Met,* won the Book World Children's Spring Book Festival Award in 1953. In 1958, *Fly*

CHUGGY AND THE BLUE CABOOSE WAS ORIGINALLY WRITTEN FOR FREEMAN'S YOUNG SON. A LOCAL LIBRARIAN SAW THE BOOK AND SUGGESTED THE FREEMANS SEND IT TO A PUBLISHER.

High, Fly Low was named a Caldecott Honor Book.

Freeman's most popular creation was a little bear in green overalls named Corduroy. Since its publication in 1968, *Corduroy* has become a classic children's book. Another book about Corduroy, *A Pocket for Corduroy,* was published in 1978, shortly after Freeman's death.

Don Freeman died on February 1, 1978, at the age of sixty-nine. Freeman's books have been translated into many foreign languages, and more than one million copies of his books are in print. They continue to delight children all over the world.

Where to Find Out More about Don Freeman

Books

Fuller, Muriel, ed. *More Junior Authors.*
New York: H. W. Wilson Company, 1963.

Something about the Author. Autobiography Series. Vol. 17.
Detroit: Gale Research, 1979.

Web Sites

Educational Paperback Association
http://www.edupaperback.org/authorbios/Freeman_Don.html
To read a biographical sketch and booklist for Don Freeman

Although Freeman lived in a rural area of California, he loved big cities.

Jean Fritz

Born: November 16, 1915

Jean Fritz loves history. She is considered to be one of the best authors of historical fiction for children and young adults. She has written more than fifty picture books, biographies, and novels during her long career. Her most famous and popular books include *And Then What Happened, Paul Revere?*, *Why Don't You Get a Horse, Sam Adams?*, and *Where Do You Think You're Going, Christopher Columbus?*

Jean Fritz was born on November 16, 1915, in Hankow, China. Her parents worked as missionaries, and she lived in China until she was about thirteen years old. As a young girl, Jean knew she wanted to be a writer. She wrote about her thoughts, ideas, and emotions in a journal.

FRITZ FOUNDED THE JEAN FRITZ WRITER'S WORKSHOPS AND TAUGHT WRITING FROM 1961 TO 1969.

As she grew up, Jean's parents told her stories about life in America. Her father also told her stories about American heroes. These stories made Jean homesick. She wanted to move to the United States. "I think it is because I was so far away that I developed a homesickness that made me want to embrace not just a given part of America at a given time but the whole of it," Fritz says.

"I get letters from readers sometimes who say they like the way I add 'fun' to history. I don't add anything. It's all true, because past times were just as filled with exciting events and 'fun' stories as are present times."

In time, Jean Fritz's family moved back to the United States. She received a degree from Wheaton College and attended Columbia University. She began her career working as a research assistant at a publishing company and as a children's librarian. She also worked as a writing teacher throughout her career.

"The question I am most often asked is 'How do I find my ideas'? The answer is, I don't. Ideas find me. A character in history will suddenly step right out of the past and demand a book."

Fritz published her first book, *Bunny Hopwell's First Spring,* in 1954. She soon published *The Cabin Faced West,* the first of several historical fiction books she has written.

JEAN FRITZ HAS WRITTEN SHORT STORIES FOR *SEVENTEEN, REDBOOK,* AND *THE NEW YORKER.*

A Selected Bibliography of Fritz's Work

The Great Little Madison (1989)
Shh! We're Writing the Constitution (1987)
The Double Life of Pocahontas (1983)
Homesick: My Own Story (1982)
Where Do You Think You're Going, Christopher Columbus? (1980)
Stonewall (1979)
Will You Sign Here, John Hancock? (1976)
Why Don't You Get a Horse, Sam Adams? (1974)
And Then What Happened, Paul Revere? (1973)
The Cabin Faced West (1958)
Bunny Hopwell's First Spring (1954)

Fritz's Major Literary Awards

1990 *Boston Globe–Horn Book* Nonfiction Award
1990 Orbis Pictus Award
The Great Little Madison

1986 Laura Ingalls Wilder Award

1984 *Boston Globe–Horn Book* Nonfiction Award
The Double Life of Pocahontas

1983 *Boston Globe–Horn Book* Fiction Honor Book
1983 National Book Award
1983 Newbery Honor Book
Homesick: My Own Story

1980 *Boston Globe–Horn Book* Nonfiction Honor Book
Stonewall

1976 *Boston Globe–Horn Book* Nonfiction Honor Book
Will You Sign Here, John Hancock?

1974 *Boston Globe–Horn Book* Fiction Honor Book
And Then What Happened, Paul Revere?

Fritz wants to make the characters come alive in her historical fiction books. She does a great deal of research for each of her books. "I like being a detective, a treasure hunter, an eavesdropper," Fritz explains. "I look for personalities whose lives make good stories." In writing her books, she refuses to use fictional dialogue for her characters. The words spoken and written by the characters in her books are taken from letters, journals, diaries, and other sources. Fritz believes that the original words make the books more real and interesting.

She has written about many people from U.S. history including George Washington, Paul Revere, Patrick Henry, and John

Hancock. Her books have also described events such as the writing of the U.S. Constitution, the Revolutionary War, and the arrival of the Pilgrims at Plymouth Rock.

Fritz lives on the Hudson River in Dobbs Ferry, New York. Her two children are now grown and live near her home. She continues to write for children and young adults.

Where to Find Out More About Jean Fritz

Books

Fritz, Jean. *China Homecoming.* New York: G. P. Putnam's Sons, 1985.

Fritz, Jean. *Homesick: My Own Story.* Waterville, Me.: Thorndike Press, 2001.

Fritz, Jean. *Surprising Myself.* Katonah, N.Y.: R. C. Owen Publishers, 1992.

Kovacs, Deborah, and James Preller. *Meet the Authors and Illustrators: 60 Creators of Favorite Children's Books Talk about Their Work.* Vol. 1. New York: Scholastic, 1991.

Web Sites

Carol Hurst's Children's Literature Site
http://www.carolhurst.com/authors/jfritz.html
To read a biographical sketch of Jean Fritz and descriptions of some of her books

Children's Book Council
http://www.cbcbooks.org/html/jeanfritz.html
To read an autobiographical sketch by Jean Fritz

In doing research for a book, Fritz often travels to where her subject was born or once lived. These trips help her to learn more about the people she is writing about.

Paul Galdone

Born: 1907
Died: November 7, 1986

Few people will ever be able to match the work of Paul Galdone. As an illustrator and writer of children's books, he completed almost 300 books during his lifetime.

Paul Galdone was born in Budapest, Hungary, in 1907. He moved to the United States as a teenager in 1921. Eventually, Galdone got the chance to study art. He studied with other young artists at the Art Students League in New York City. Then Galdone enrolled at the New York School of Industrial Design.

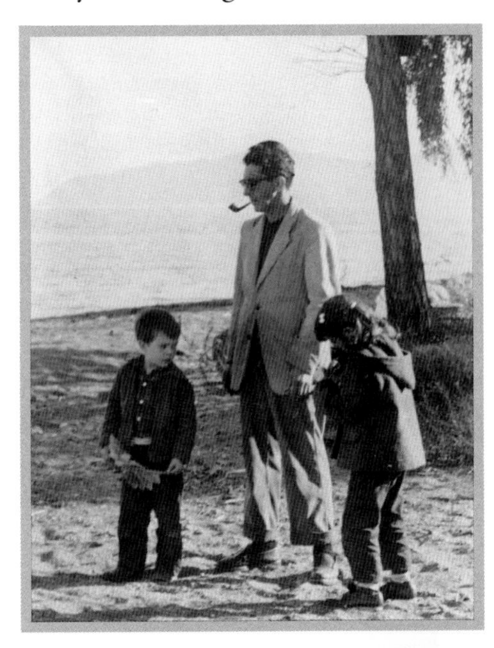

When Paul Galdone finished his studies, he began his career in the art department of a book publisher in New York City. He used the skills he learned there for the rest of his life. Galdone learned how artists, authors, and editors

PAUL GALDONE ILLUSTRATED A WIDE VARIETY OF BOOKS, INCLUDING A BOOK OF KNOCK-KNOCK JOKES AND A STORY FROM THE BIBLE.

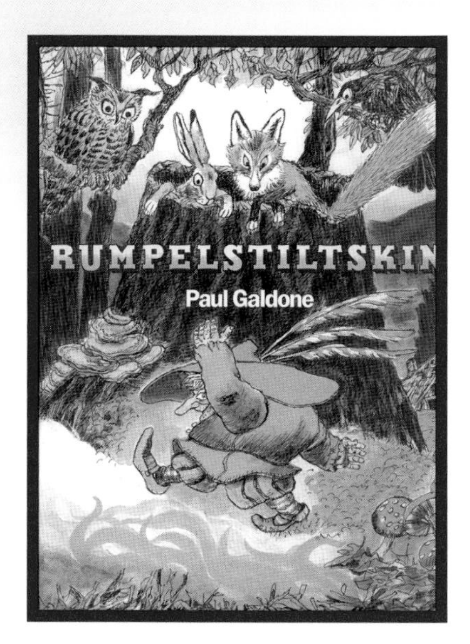

work together, how pages are laid out, and how books are produced.

At his job, Galdone designed and illustrated book covers and dust jackets, many of them for adult readers. His cover illustrations appeared on books by Mark Twain, Jane Austen, Edgar Allan Poe, and Charles Dickens. For this work, he used bold lettering and dramatic images very different from his

A Selected Bibliography of Galdone's Work

Nursery Classics: A Golden Treasury (2001)
Cat Goes Fiddle-I-Fee (1985)
Rumpelstiltskin (1985)
The Elves and the Shoemaker (1984)
The Monster and the Tailor: A Ghost Story (1982)
The Turtle and the Monkey (1983)
Insects All around Us (Illustrations only, 1981)
King of the Cats: A Ghost Story (1980)
Anatole and the Pied Piper (Illustrations only, 1979)
Zed and the Monsters (Illustrations only, 1979)
Puss in Boots (1976)
The Gingerbread Boy (1975)
The Queen Who Couldn't Bake Gingerbread (Illustrations only, 1975)
The Three Billy Goats Gruff (Illustrations only, 1973)
Basil and the Pygmy Cats; a Basil of Baker Street Mystery (Illustrations only, 1971)
Anatole and the Thirty Thieves (Illustrations only, 1969)
The Hairy Horror Trick (Illustrations only, 1969)
Whiskers, My Cat (Illustrations only, 1967)
The Hare and the Tortoise (Illustrations only, 1962)
The Disappearing Dog Trick (Illustrations only, 1961)
Old Mother Hubbard and Her Dog (Illustrations only, 1960)
Bascombe, the Fastest Hound Alive (Illustrations only, 1958)
Anatole and the Cat (Illustrations only, 1957)
Anatole (Illustrations only, 1956)
Nine Lives; or, the Celebrated Cat of Beacon Hill (Illustrations only, 1951)

Galdone's Major Literary Awards

1958 Caldecott Honor Book
Anatole and the Cat

1957 Caldecott Honor Book
Anatole

> *"What will you give me," said the little man, "if I spin this straw into gold for you?"*
> —*from* Rumpelstiltskin

children's illustrations.

During World War II (1939–1945), Paul Galdone worked in the art department of the U.S. Army Corps of Engineers. After his military service, Galdone began illustrating books for children.

For children just beginning to read, Galdone illustrated the Anatole and Basil books, both written by Eve Titus. Anatole is a French mouse who cleverly solves problems faced by his mouse friends. Basil is a British mouse who solves mysteries. Galdone's charming mouse pictures are in black and white, with the occasional one or two colors added.

Galdone also illustrated many books for older children. Among his most popular books are those relating the adventures of Kerby Maxwell. Books written by Scott Corbett such as *The Hairy Horror Trick* and *The Disappearing Dog Trick* include many pen-and-ink illustrations of Kerby and his friend Fenton.

Throughout his life, Paul Galdone had a special interest in fables. He gathered tales from around the world, and then retold and illustrated them. He published stories from Germany, Russia, India, Puerto Rico, and the Philippines. One such story is *The Turtle and the Monkey.* This fable tells of a turtle who needs help getting a banana tree out of the

---

Paul Galdone held many jobs during his life. Early positions included bus boy, electrician's helper, and fur dryer!

river. She succeeds in getting the monkey to help her but comes to regret his assistance when he grows greedy and asks for more fruit than he deserves. He also retold and illustrated tales from the Brothers Grimm, Hans Christian Andersen, and Aesop. Galdone's exciting pictures bring to life ancient fables such as Aesop's *The Hare and the Tortoise.* This story explains how a slow but determined tortoise wins the race over the quick but foolish hare.

"Today I brew, tomorrow I bake. The next day, the young Queen's child I'll take. Soon far and wide will spread the fame that Rumpelstiltskin is my name."
—*from* Rumpelstiltskin

Paul Galdone enjoyed illustrating for people of all ages. He died of a heart attack on November 7, 1986, leaving behind a collection of work that children and adults will enjoy for years to come.

Where to Find Out More about Paul Galdone

Books

Collier, Laurie, and Joyce Nakamura, eds. *Major Authors and Illustrators for Children and Young Adults: A Selection of Sketches from Something about the Author.* Detroit: Gale Research, 1993.

McElmeel, Sharron L. *100 Most Popular Picture Book Authors and Illustrators.* Englewood, Colo.: Libraries Unlimited, 2000.

Web Sites

Paul Galdone's Modern Library Dust Jackets
http://www.dogeared.com/Identifiers/artists/galdoneJackets.html
To see book jackets for the classics designed by Galdone

Jack Gantos

Born: July 2, 1951

Jack Gantos became interested in becoming a writer by writing in a diary. At first, he wrote in a diary because that's what his sister did. She was older, and he liked to imitate her. Over time, Gantos began using his diary to keep track of things that were important to him. This interest in writing was enough to help Gantos begin his career as a writing teacher and children's author. He is best known as the author of the Rotten Ralph series. He has also written other picture books for children, as well as novels for young people.

Jack Gantos was born on July 2, 1951, in Mount Pleasant, Pennsylvania. Jack was in second grade when he told his mother he wanted a

---

MANY OF THE ROTTEN RALPH BOOKS HAVE BEEN PUBLISHED IN HEBREW AND JAPANESE.

diary like his sister. His mother finally agreed to get him a diary. She told him that he had to write in it every day. He would sit next to his sister and write in his diary. He would also try to peek at what his sister was writing. "When she caught me, she just laughed," Gantos says. "'Go ahead and look' she said and showed me her diary." He could not read what his sister had written because she wrote in French!

> *"I still read and write in my journal every day."*

A few years later, Jack's family was planning to move to Barbados, an island in the Caribbean Sea. Jack's mother told him that he could only bring his books and diaries when they moved. He did not know what to do because he had collected many baseball cards, stamps, marbles, rocks, and butterflies that he wanted to keep. Jack figured out ways to put many of these things in his diaries. "By the time we were ready to move, I had put all of my junk into all of my diaries," Gantos says. "My mother was very surprised, but because my junk was now so well organized, she let me bring it."

Jack Gantos continued writing in his journals through high school and college. When he was a student at Emerson College in Boston, he met an art student who did illustrations. Gantos decided to begin writing children's books.

GANTOS ATTENDED TEN DIFFERENT SCHOOLS WHEN HE WAS GROWING UP.

A Selected Bibliography of Gantos's Work

Hole in My Life (2002)
Practice Makes Perfect for Rotten Ralph (2002)
What Would Joey Do? (2002)
Rotten Ralph Helps Outs (2001)
Joey Pigza Loses Control (2000)
Wedding Bells for Rotten Ralph (1999)
Back to School for Rotten Ralph (1998)
Joey Pigza Swallowed the Key (1998)
Rotten Ralph's Halloween Howl (1998)
Desire Lines (1997)
Jack's Black Book (1997)
Rotten Ralph's Rotten Romance (1997)
Jack's New Power: Stories from a Caribbean Year (1995)
Heads or Tails: Stories from the Sixth Grade (1994)
Not So Rotten Ralph (1994)
Happy Birthday, Rotten Ralph (1990)
Rotten Ralph's Show and Tell (1989)
Rotten Ralph's Trick or Treat! (1986)
Swampy Alligator (1980)
The Werewolf Family (1980)
Willy's Raiders (1980)
The Perfect Pal (1979)
Worse Than Rotten, Ralph (1978)
Fair-Weather Friends (1977)
Sleepy Ronald (1976)
Rotten Ralph (1976)

Gantos's Major Literary Awards

2001 Newbery Honor Book
Joey Pigza Loses Control

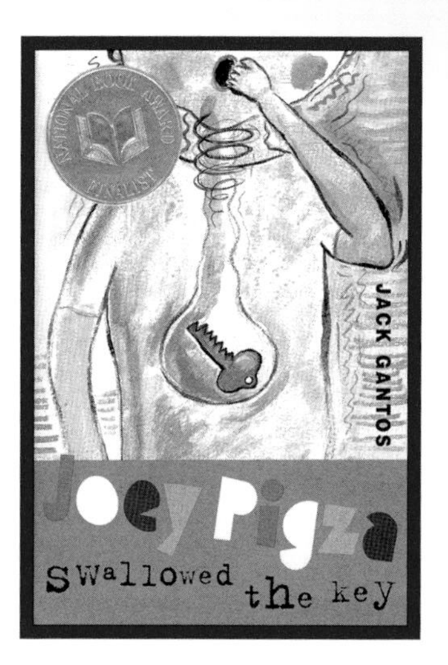

The first book Gantos wrote was rejected because the publisher said it was boring. But then Gantos remembered that a teacher once told him to write about things that he were familiar. "I looked down at the floor and saw my lousy, grumpy, hissing creep of a cat that loved to scratch my ankles, throw fur around the house, and shred my clothes in my closet," Gantos says. The cat was the inspiration for his first children's book,

Rotten Ralph, published in 1976. He went on to write many more books in the Rotten Ralph series.

Along with writing for children, Gantos teaches courses in children's book writing at Vermont College. He also travels around the country to speak at schools, libraries, and writing conferences.

> *"I enjoy my work as much as possible. I read good books and I want to write good books."*

Where to Find Out More about Jack Gantos

Books

Gantos, Jack. *Hole in My Life.* New York: Farrar, Straus, and Giroux, 2002.

Holtze, Sally Holmes, ed. *Fifth Book of Junior Authors & Illustrators.* New York: H. W. Wilson Company, 1983.

Web Sites

KidsReads.com
http://www.kidsreads.com/reviews/0374399891.asp
To read a synopsis and review for Newbery Honor Book *Joey Pigza Loses Control*

LD Online: Exclusive Interview with Jack Gantos
http://www.ldonline.org/kidzone/books_excerpt/joey_key_interview.html
To read an interview with Jack Gantos and excerpts from *Joey Pigza Swallowed the Key*

In the novel *Heads or Tails: Stories from the Sixth Grade,* Gantos talks about growing up with his sister and moving with his family.

INDEX

NOTE TO READERS: *In this multivolume index, the number before the colon indicates the volume in which that entry appears, and the number following the colon is the page within the volume.*

A

B

C

G

H

O

P